Disorders of
Sexual Desire

CLINICAL INSIGHTS

COMPREHENSIVE EVALUATION OF
Disorders of Sexual Desire

Edited by
HELEN SINGER KAPLAN, M.D., Ph.D.

Director, Human Sexuality Program, The New York Hospital-Cornell Medical Center; and Clinical Professor of Psychiatry, Cornell University Medical College

AMERICAN PSYCHIATRIC PRESS, INC.
Washington, D.C.

Note: The authors have worked to ensure that all information in this book concerning drug dosages, schedules, and routes of administration is accurate at the time of publication and consistent with standards set by the U.S. Food and Drug Administration and the general medical community. As medical research and practice advance, however, therapeutic standards may change. For this reason and because human and mechanical errors sometimes occur, we recommend that readers follow the advice of a physician directly involved in their care or the care of a member of their family.

Library of Congress Cataloging in Publication Data

Main entry under title:
Comprehensive evaluation of disorders of sexual desire.
  (Clinical insights)
  Half-title: Disorders of sexual desire.
  1. Psychosexual disorders—Diagnosis. I. Kaplan, Helen Singer, 1929–
II. Title: Disorders of sexual desire. III. Series. [DNLM: 1. Psychosexual
Disorders. WM 610 C737]
RC556.C63   1985   616.85′83   84-18625
ISBN 0-88048-066-1 (pbk.)

Printed in the U.S.A.

Contents

Contributors

JOSHUA S. GOLDEN, M.D.
Professor of Psychiatry and Director, Human Sexuality Program,
University of California at Los Angeles

HELEN SINGER KAPLAN, M.D., Ph.D.
Director, Human Sexuality Program, The New York Hospital-
Cornell Medical Center; and Clinical Professor of Psychiatry,
Cornell University Medical College

OTTO F. KERNBERG, M.D.
Medical Director, The New York Hospital-Cornell Medical Center,
Westchester Division; Professor of Psychiatry, Cornell University Medical
College; and Training and Supervising Analyst, Columbia University Center
for Psychoanalytic Training and Research

HAROLD I. LIEF, M.D.
Professor of Psychiatry, University of Pennsylvania School of Medicine;
and Psychiatrist at the Pennsylvania Hospital

RAUL C. SCHIAVI, M.D.
Director, Human Sexuality Program, The Mount Sinai Medical Center;
and Professor of Psychiatry, Mount Sinai Medical College

1

Comprehensive Evaluation of Disorders of Sexual Desire: Introduction and Overview

Helen Singer Kaplan, M.D., Ph.D.

1

Comprehensive Evaluation of Disorders of Sexual Desire: Introduction and Overview

Disorders of sexual desire are probably the most prevalent of all the sexual dysfunctions. Dr. Harold Lief, who has been a leader in the recognition and understanding of this syndrome, has estimated that approximately 40 percent of the patients who seek help for sexual difficulties at his program for marital and sexual therapy in Philadelphia suffer from impairment of their sex drive. The experience of other centers that evaluate and treat patients with sexual complaints, including our own in New York City, is similar. However, the consideration of low desire state as a distinct clinical entity is new. Until the recent past, deficiencies in the sex drive were not recognized as such and these disorders were subsumed under the labels "impotence" or "frigidity." This syndrome did not appear in the official nomenclature until 1980, when it was included in DSM-III under the category of Psychosexual Dysfunction.

The creation of this new nosological entity was not a meaningless theoretical exercise. There are compelling practical reasons for classifying desire disorders in a separate diagnostic category. Impairment of the sex drive is associated with a specific set of causes related to but different from the physical and psychological stressors that cause disorders of the orgasm and excitement phases of the human sexual response. A summary of the clinical features of the sexual dysfunctions and some common psychological and organic causes is shown in Table 1. As a consequence of these differences, impaired desire states are amenable to different and specific treatment strategies and also carry a less favorable prognosis. Patients with inhibited sexual desire (ISD) are likely to suffer from more severe and complex psychological and relationship problems than those with psychogenic genital phase dysfunctions (1, 2). In my experience, only a small proportion of the patients whose desire is inhibited respond to brief, behaviorally oriented sex therapy alone. In addition to specially structured sexual experiences, the typical case requires a greater degree of emphasis on insight into and resolution of intrapsychic sexual conflicts and difficulties in the couple's relationship.

Impaired sexual desire is one of those multidetermined pathological states in which identical symptoms can be produced by a wide range of biological and psychological etiologies. Therefore, precise evaluation of the causal factors is a prerequisite for successful treatment. Many treatment failures can be traced to the clinician's lack of understanding of the differential diagnosis of this syndrome or the failure to diagnose the essential causes correctly.

RULING OUT BIOLOGICAL CAUSES: AGE, DEPRESSION, ILLNESS, AND DRUGS

It is the first and foremost task of the evaluation to detect patients whose sex drive is impaired by disease states or drugs before there can be any consideration of psychological treatment. When a patient totally loses desire and develops a complete "sexual anorexia," it is mandatory to rule out certain organic factors. This is less critical when desire is lost selectively. For example, if desire is lost only for the spouse and the patient is able to respond to other partners or to erotic fantasies, a situational loss of libido is more likely to be psychogenic. It should be cautioned, however, that slowly progressive medical disorders may at first appear to be situational as the patient attempts to compensate for a diminishing sex drive by enlisting especially arousing psychic stimulation.

Table 1   The Sexual Dysfunctions: Physiology, Clinical Features, and Causes[a]

	Male	Female
1. Orgasm Phase Disorders		
The Physiology of Orgasm	*Phase 1—Emission:* contraction of smooth muscles or internal male reproductive organs collects ejaculate in the posterior urethra	No female emission phase[b]
	*Phase 2—*Ejaculation: 0.8/sec. contractions of striated perineal muscles, propels semen out of urethra. Pleasurable.	*Phase 2—*Orgasm: 0.8/sec. contractions of striated perineal muscles; pleasurable
Clinical Features	*Premature ejaculation (PE):* inadequate control of ejaculation reflex	No clinical female analogue
	Retarded ejaculation (RE): delayed or absent ejaculation	Inhibited female orgasm; delayed or absent orgasm
	Partial retarded ejaculation: inhibition of emission phase only; no pleasure	"Missed" female orgasm

Common Organic Causes	1) There are no *common* organic causes of primary ejaculatory disorders
	2) Secondary ejaculatory disorders:
	  a) radical abdominal and pelvic surgery; trauma and diseases of the lower spinal cord
	  b) alpha adrenergic blocking drugs; thioridazine
		1) There are no *common* organic causes of primary anorgasmia
		2) Secondary anorgasmia:
		  a) advanced diabetes
		  b) MAO inhibitor drugs

Psychological Causes	*PE:* failure to perceive or register erotic sensations premonitory to orgasm	

Table 1 *(continued)*

	Male	Female
A) Immediate Causes	*RE* (and partial RE): 1) Obsessive self-observation during sex 2) inability to "let go"	*Inhibited female orgasm:* 1) obsessive self-observation during sex 2) inability to "let go" 3) insufficient stimulation
B) Deeper Intrapsychic and Relationship Causes	*PE:* tend to be mild *RE:* variable—sometimes associated with hostility towards women	*Inhibited female orgasm:* tend to be mild

2. Excitement Phase Disorders

Physiology of Excitement	*Genital Vasocongestion:* Dilation of penile arteries increases inflow of blood, while outflow is diminished. This creates a high pressure system in the cavernous sinuses of the penis which produces *erection.*	*Genital Vasocongestion:* Diffuse dilation of blood vessels in labia and around vagina produces *genital swelling* and *vaginal lubrication.*
Clinical Features	Impotence	Vaginal dryness, Painful coitus
Common Organic Causes	1) Diabetes 2) Penile circulatory problems 3) Endocrine problems (low testosterone, high prolactin) 4) Drugs: antihypertensives, beta blockers, alcohol	Estrogen deficiency (menopause)
Psychological Causes		
A) Immediate Causes	Performance anxiety Partner pressure Overconcern with pleasing partner	?

Table 1 *(continued)*

	Male	Female
B) Deeper Causes	Not specific—vary from mild performance anxiety to severe neurosis *Intrapsychic*—oedipal problems, cultural guilt about sex *Relationship*—ambivalence towards partner, overconcern with pleasing partner, fear of rejection	Ambivalence about intercourse

3. Desire Phase Disorders

	Male	Female
Physiology of Desire	Activation of sex circuits in brain—mediated by *testosterone.*	Same as male, requires lower level of testosterone.
Clinical Features	1) Total loss of desire 2) Loss of desire in specific situation only	Same
Common Organic Causes	1) Disease states that reduce testosterone 2) Depression 3) Severe stress 4) Drugs that impair the sex circuits of the brain: beta blockers, narcotics, alcohol	Same
Psychological Causes		
A) Immediate Causes	1) "Anti-fantasies"—focus on negative aspects of partner or sexual situation 2) Avoidance of erotic stimulation 3) Avoidance of erotic fantasies	Same
B) Deeper Causes	Often severe, not specific 1) *Intrapsychic*—fear of intimacy and commitment 2) *Relationship*—anger at partner	Same

Table 1 *(continued)*

	Male	Female
4. Sexual Disorders Associated with Genital Muscle Spasm		
Clinical Features	Ejaculatory pain—secondary avoidance	Vaginismus—dyspareunia + secondary avoidance
Common Organic Causes	Infections of the urogenital tract, e.g., prostatis, vesiculitis, herpes, etc.	Painful gynecologic conditions, e.g., pelvic inflammatory disease, endometriosis, hymenal obstruction, painful hymenal remnants, herpes, etc.
Pathology	Conditioned involuntary painful spasm of cremasteric or perineal muscles or muscles of internal reproductive organs	Conditioned involuntary spasm of the circumvaginal muscles
Psychological Causes	Ambivalence about ejaculating	Variable—ranges from simple conditioned guarding reaction to severe neurosis and relationship problems

5. Functional Dyspareunia

	Male	Female
Clinical Features	Pain on erection, intromission or ejaculation	Pain on entry, deep thrusting, orgasm
Organic Causes	Pain is *more often organic than psychogenic* and organic cause must be ruled out in each case	Same
Psychological Mechanisms (Psychogenic Dyspareunia)	1) Hypochondriacal overreaction to normal sensations 2) Hysterical pain 3) Pain-depression syndrome 4) Intractable schizophrenic pain 5) Functional genital muscle spasm 6) Brutal sexual intercourse	Same Also, vaginismus

Table 1 *(continued)*

	Male	Female
6. Phobic Avoidance of Sex		
Clinical Features	Phobic avoidance of sex	Same
Cause	1) Associated with panic disorder	Same
	2) Simple sexual phobia—conditioning and neurotic processes	

[a] From Kaplan HS: The Evaluation of Sexual Disorders: Psychological and Medical Aspects. New York, Brunner/Mazel, 1983. Reprinted with permission.
[b] Claims for "female ejaculation" have not been substantiated.

Age

The most common organic cause of diminished sexual desire is the aging process. People who are in good health with healthy partners can enjoy sex until the end of their days, but the sex drive and sexual ability does decline, especially in men, as a normal aspect of the aging process. The normal age-related decline is only partial and can be overcome by healthy couples with open sexual attitudes. If these changes are misunderstood by the patient or by the partner, however, a premature and unnecessary asexuality can result, with its sequellae of marital problems, depression, stress, and stress-related disease states. Therapeutic intervention can be very helpful in such cases (3).

Depression and Stress

Depression and stress are included here because the sex drive is impaired in depression on a psychophysiologic basis, independently of intrapsychic sexual conflicts or marital difficulties. In fact, depression is the single most common cause of global loss of sexual desire in young persons. Changes in libido may occur before mood changes and are a common sign of a masked depression.

Disease States

Physicians have long recognized that severe disease and profound endocrine deficiency states will depress a patient's sex drive. However, the appreciation of the sexual effects of many of the less obvious diseases and of many medications is a new trend in medicine just now coming to the attention of the medical profession. Even though a patient has been referred by the physician with the assurance that there are no medical problems, it is still incumbent on the clinician who evaluates sexual disorders to be aware of the fact that there are many subtle disease states not usually detected by routine medical and urological or gynecologic examinations that may, in fact, lower a person's sex drive. These include subtle testosterone deficiencies and dysfunctions of the hypophyseal-gonadal axis, slowly growing prolactin-secreting tumors of the pituitary gland, diabetes (even in its early stages), and atherosclerotic changes in the penile vasculature. Unfortunately, such medical disorders may have no other signs and symptoms apart from a loss of sexual interest. For these reasons, it is my practice to guard against erroneous medical clearance by screening all patients who complain of low desire for such conditions with a simple battery of specialized tests. Apart from protecting patients from being subjected to inappropriate and ineffective psychological treatment, the detection of subtle but potentially dangerous disease states and referral for appropriate medical treatment is an important and valuable function of the clinician who evaluates sexual complaints.

Drugs

Among medications in common use that may affect sexual functions are alcohol, narcotics, high doses of certain psychoactive medications, beta-adrenergic blockers used to treat and prevent heart disease, and some of the centrally acting antihypertensive agents. For these reasons, no evaluation of this syndrome is complete without questioning the patient about the use of medications and substance abuse. In Chapter 2, Dr. Raul Schiavi describes the more common organic causes of reduced libido and also discusses methods of evaluating these.

ASSESSING PSYCHOLOGICAL CAUSES

Although the importance of ruling out biological causes cannot be overemphasized, the majority of complaints of low or absent sexual desire have a psychogenic basis. The accurate analysis of the psychological causes is the primary and most challenging aspect of the evaluation, and the key to successful treatment results.

Psychological determinants may be divided into intrapsychic sexual conflicts and pathological interactions with the sexual partner. Patients with inner psychosexual conflicts have sexual difficulties even with supportive and attractive lovers. In other cases of ISD neither partner has an intrinsic sexual inhibition, but the symptom originates in the couple's problematic relationship.

Intrapsychic Causes: Maladaptive Sexual Behavior, Neurotic Processes, Antisexual Cultural Indoctrination, and Sexual Phobias

Immediate Causes. The metaphor of "layers" of psycho-pathology is useful for conceptualizing the evaluation and treatment of patients with sexual disorders (1, 2). According to this concept, the "immediate" psychological causes of ISD are currently operating maladaptive behaviors or psychic events, and mental processes that impair sexual pleasure and performance in the "here and now."

Maladaptive sexual behaviors are invariably implicated in ISD. The most commonly seen "immediate" causes in this patient population include: (a) performance anxiety, which may or may not be associated with sexual dysfunction; (b) partner pressure or lack of support; (c) inadequate physical and mental stimulation; and (d) the conscious suppression of sexual fantasies. Another extremely important defense seen in this syndrome are self-induced negative mental states wherein the patient focuses on unpleasant aspects of the partner or on anxiety-arousing extraneous matters such as taxes or stressful responsibilities, with the result that sexual desire is diminished (1). Typically, ISD patients show no resistance to recognizing these sexually self-sabotaging behavioral defenses but have no insight into their deeper psychic significance.

An important and often overlooked cause of diminished sexual interest and frequency is the phobic avoidance of sex. Such patients panic in sexual situations and therefore avoid and suppress sexual feelings. Sexual avoidance may occur as a simple phobia, but more often is a symptom of a generalized panic disorder. The clinical importance of detecting panic-prone patients during the evaluation lies in the fact that their prognosis improves significantly when antipanic medication is added to the treatment regimen.

In my experience, ISD cannot be cured unless the maladaptive behavior responsible for the sexual impairment is corrected. It is a basic strategy of the new sex therapies to use specific behavioral interventions to accomplish this objective. For this reason, the evaluation of patients with low sexual desire cannot be considered complete unless a detailed analysis of the patient's maladaptive, sexually sabotaging behavior is included and the "immediate causes" of the sexual inhibition are clearly understood. In Chapter 3, Dr. Joshua Golden describes the assessment of ISD patients' current sexual experience, and the clinical significance of this information.

Deeper Intrapsychic Causes and Neurotic Processes

Antisexual cultural messages. Among patients with orgasm and erection phase problems, it is quite common to find that the primary causal factors are consciously perceived behavioral defenses against sex, of the kind described above, with no evidence of underlying major psychopathology or serious marital disorder. Although such relatively "minor" sexual conflicts are also the only or critical determinant of blocked desire in a small proportion of ISD patients, more often patients with desire disorders also have significant underlying conflicts about sexual pleasure, love, and intimacy that derive from unconscious psychodynamic processes. For purposes of evaluation and treatment, it is useful to divide these into culturally derived antisexual attitudes and neurotic processes, which have their origin in the patient's pathological childhood development.

According to the "levels of causation" metaphor, these intrapsychic conflicts are considered in the category of "deeper" causes. The most common of these found in ISD are culturally induced attitudes of sexual guilt and shame, unconscious intrapsychic sexual conflicts, and a fear of intimacy and commitment, which makes it difficult for the individual to blend erotic and tender feelings.

Highly traditional and devoutly religious Christian and Jewish families may transmit to their children the message that sex is wrong and sinful, that "good girls don't," and that sexual thoughts and acts are "impure." These cultural attitudes are internalized and can hamper the free expression of the individual's sexuality throughout life even when the person is basically healthy emotionally and involved in a good relationship.

Neurotic processes also create conflicts about sex and interfere with sexual feelings and functioning by evoking disruptive anxiety when the patient tries to make love. These processes are the product of childhood maladaptation to family pathology and can occur in the most liberal families. There are various sensible ways of conceptualizing the neurotic intrapsychic conflicts that impair the sex drive. Many clinicians find that psychoanalytic concepts provide especially useful insights into otherwise puzzling sexual difficulties, including many cases of ISD.

According to psychoanalytic theory, sexual conflicts arising out of unresolved issues from the oedipal period of development may create inner conflicts about sex and a variety of sexual disorders, including ISD. These patients unconsciously regard their sexual partners as parents, which taints the sexual act with incestuous taboos. More serious psychopathology, believed to originate in childhood trauma from the preoedipal period, is implicated in other cases of ISD. These patients suffer from personality disorders that are marked, along with various other psychological difficulties, by a lack of the capacity to love or to sustain erotic feelings within a permanent caring relationship. Analytic constructs can be extremely valuable for providing a rational therapeutic structure for working with these more serious sexual difficulties, which are often refractory to rapid behaviorally oriented approaches, and which present difficult clinical problems.

Dr. Otto Kernberg has done major work in the psychopathology of love and sex. Chapter 4 discusses the evaluation of the ISD patients with neurotic sexual conflicts and with personality disorders from a psychoanalytic perspective.

Relationship Problems: Inadequate Sexual Interactions, Poor Communications, Power Struggles, Mutual Transferences, Incompatible Marriage

Chapter 5 describes relationship problems regarded by many clinicians as the most important determinants of ISD. Difficulties in the couple's sexual and emotional system play such a significant role in psychosexual disorders that Masters and Johnson have stated that "the couple is the patient" (4). This is in sharp contrast with the traditional psychoanalytic position, which holds that sexual psychopathology resides solely within the psyche of the symptomatic patient to the extent that in psychoanalysis only the patient is seen, and the partner is not involved in the treatment process at all.

Both kinds of cases exist. A significant number of patients cannot sustain erotic feelings in any intimate or committed relationship and lose their sexual interest with all partners, even the most attractive and supportive ones. More frequently, however, both partners have the capacity for love and sex under some conditions, but are inhibited because there are specific problems in the current relationship. Sexual desire may become suppressed because of difficulties in a couple's sexual interactions only, within the context of an otherwise sound and loving relationship.

Table 2 Evaluation of ISD

Ruling Out Biological Causes

Rule out impaired desire due to disease states and drugs with sexual side effects

Method: medical history + medication survey;

screen: physical examination + testosterone, LH, FSH, prolactin, estradiole, thyroid studies, glycohemoglobin

Rule our ISD secondary to major and treatable psychiatric disorders: depression, stress + panic disorder

Method: psyciatric evaluation of both partners

Analysis of Psychological Causes

Assessment of currently operating defenses against sexual pleasure (immediate causes)

Method: detailed examination of couple's curent sexual experience (sexual status)

Assessment of unconscious intrapsychic sexual conflicts of both partners (deeper causes)

Method: family + psychosexual histories, include evaluation of family dynamics + "sexual messages"

Assessment of relationship causes

Method: examine current relationship in its sexual and nonsexual aspects and review history of romantic object relations of both partners.

In other cases, the sexual relationship is adequate in terms of providing sufficient mental and physical stimulation for both partners, but one or both do not feel desire despite this and they avoid sex with each other because of difficulties in the non-erotic aspects in their life together.

Anger at the partner for any reason is probably the most common cause of inhibited sexual desire. It is difficult to desire a person with whom one is furious, or to allow oneself to be vulnerable in a relationship devoid of trust. Anger is the final common pathway of a variety of pathological processes. These range from realistic disillusionment and disappointments with the partner, to intermeshing neurotic processes that cause spouses to develop regressive infantile reactions toward each other, which are incompatible with a pleasurable adult sexual response. Sometimes the evaluation of a couple who seek consultation for lack of sexual interest reveals a relationship that is so incompatible that it makes no sense to try to improve their sexual interactions. Such persons need clarification and resolution of their marital problems and not sex therapy.

There are various useful ways of conceptualizing pathological systems that can impair sexual desire. Dr. Harold Lief has done pioneering work in the area of sex and marriage and has described the pathological dynamics that may impair desire in highly innovative and clinically useful terms. Chapter 5 deals with relationship causes of sexual desire disorders and the methods used to evaluate these.

A COMPREHENSIVE APPROACH TO EVALUATION

The separation of these four classes of causes is, of course, artificial and was done primarily for didactic purposes. In reality, biological intrapsychic and dyadic problems merge and meld in complex ways to impair the patient's sexual desire. Thus the neurotic patient uses the dictates of the church in the service of uncon-

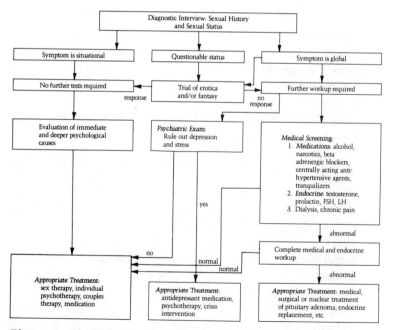

Figure 1 The Evaluation of Low or Absent Sexual Desire. From Kaplan HS: The Evaluation of Sexual Disorders: Psychological and Medical Aspects. New York, Brunner/Mazel, 1983. Reprinted with permission.

scious sexual conflict. A couple's marital battles reflect a meshing of their individual psychopathologies as they act out their infantile jealousies and angers with each other. Unresolved developmental issues emerge in such marriages and marital sex becomes symbolically an incestuous act. The partial, biologically determined diminution of an elderly man's sexual capacity may tap into his latent insecurities and a minor problem is escalated into a total and unnecessary asexuality. An angry, disillusioned wife may subtly withdraw the support her diabetic husband needs, and the discouraged husband may retreat into an asexual mode (3).

Because sexual desire depends on the balance of many elements and can be disturbed by multiple stressors, the evaluation of each case must encompass the assessment of all of these elements—with a view toward rational and specific therapeutic interventions.

It is useful to organize the evaluation of the patient and the couple who complain of deficient sexual desire according to the system depicted in Figure 1. Table 2 presents a summary of the data required to evaluate ISD and the clinical methods used to obtain the data.

References

1. Kaplan HS: Disorders of Sexual Desire. New York, Brunner/Mazel, 1979

2. Kaplan HS: Evaluation of Sexual Disorders: Psychological and Medical Aspects. New York, Brunner/Mazel, 1983

3. Kaplan HS: Sexual relationships in middle-age. Physician & Patient, October 1983

4. Masters WM, Johnson V: Human Sexual Inadequacy. Boston, Little, Brown, 1970

2

Evaluation of Impaired Sexual Desire: Biological Aspects

Raul C. Schiavi, M.D.

2

Evaluation of Impaired Sexual Desire: Biological Aspects

Although it is clear that organic causes can diminish the human sex drive, and a rich pool of clinical description is available, there is limited empirical information on psychobiological factors associated with loss of sexual desire. Conceptually, a major source of difficulty has been a failure to distinguish clearly among sexual desire, arousal, activity, responsiveness, and satisfaction. Some of the methodological problems in the investigation of sexual desire have included inadequately described subject groups, the use of unreliable hormonal and behavioral assessments, and lack of appropriate controls. In recent years, significant biological information relevant to our understanding of sexual desire has begun to emerge. The most salient aspects of these data will be briefly reviewed before focusing on disordered behavior.

PSYCHOBIOLOGY OF SEXUAL DESIRE

The prevailing notion that androgens play a critical role in male sexual drive has been substantiated by recent double-blind studies in hypogonadal men (1-3). Androgen withdrawal resulted in a rapid decrease in sexual interest accompanied by a reduction in sexual activity; replacement therapy lead to a significant increase in sexual thoughts and a reestablishment of sexual desire within

18

two weeks. It is of note that erectile capacity measured by responsiveness to erotic films was not affected by androgen withdrawal. This observation, replicated in two different laboratories (3, 4), suggests that androgens may be more important, at least on a short-term basis, to maintain sexual desire than erectile capacity.

In women, the weight of current evidence, primarily derived from studies on hormonal variations during the menstrual cycle (5–7), also suggests that endogenous androgens play a significant role in sexual desire and activity. The effects of androgens on sexual function do not seem to be solely due to nonspecific effects on energy levels and mood. It is not clear, however, whether androgens influence sexual desire by a central effect on cognitive processes such as fantasy production (8), by a peripheral action enhancing genital sensitivity and pleasurable awareness of sexual responses (9), or by an interplay of both elements.

The main circulating androgens are testosterone in both sexes and androstendione produced by the ovaries and the adrenal cortex in women. Only a small fraction (about 5 percent in men) is free and presumed to be physiologically active at the target cell level; the remainder is bound to plasma proteins. Current evidence, primarily from animal studies (9), suggests that testosterone requires conversion to dihydrotestosterone and estradiol to exert physiological and behavioral effects. The role of these peripheral transformations in the modulation of human sexual desire requires study.

Prolactin, luteinizing hormone-releasing hormone, and endorphins have also been implicated in changes in sexual desire (8, 10). The physiological significance of these observations derived mainly from pathological conditions or pharmacological interventions is still not clear.

It is believed based primarily on animal experimentation that the behavioral effects of gonadal hormones are mediated by steroid-sensitive structures located within the hypothalamic-limbic system. Recent studies have begun to delineate an interaction among dopaminergic, serotonergic, and cholinergic systems in the control of sexual interest and behavior (11). In animal studies, enhanced dopaminergic activities tend to increase sexual activity, whereas activation of the serotonergic system decreases sexual beahavior. Drugs that block synthesis of serotonin, such as p-chloromethamphetamine, increase sexual activity in the presence of androgen (12). Generalizations to human behavior, of course, are presently tentative at best.

PSYCHOBIOLOGICAL DETERMINANTS OF DECREASED SEXUAL DESIRE

Sexual desire may be influenced by naturally occurring physiologic processes such as aging and pregnancy. It may also be disturbed by pathological and iatrogenic conditions such as medical illness, a wide range of pharmacological agents, and mood disorders.

Natural Processes

Aging. Several studies have documented a decrease in sexual activity and an increase prevalence of sexual difficulties in aging men (13–15). Some investigators (16, 17), not all (18), have reported a lowering in circulating testosterone and a compensatory increase in luteinizing hormone gradually developing with advancing age. It has been speculated, but not until recently experimentally assessed, that changes in androgen secretion are responsible for the decline in sexual interest and activity in older men. In a large cross-sectional study, Davidson et al. (19) were able to confirm that total and free testosterone decrease with age and that these changes correlate with a reduction in sexual desire and activity. Hormonal factors, however, accounted for only a small part of the age-related decrease in sexual functioning.

Although Davidson et al. (19) did not observe a relation between prolactin and sexual activity, Weizman et al. (20) recently found that elderly healthy men who had decreased sexual drive had significantly higher prolactin levels than a comparable group of men without desire changes. It needs to be emphasized that a wide range in sexual desire and activity as well as in hormonal levels is usually found within each age cohort. Even within the 70 to 80 age range, there are subjects who show a degree of sexual interest and activity that is comparable to much younger age groups.

In women, there is a decrease in ovarian response to gonadotropins preceding and following menopause, with considerable individual postmenopausal variations in circulating estrogens. For example, McLennan and McLennan (21) found that 40 percent of postmenopausal women had adequately estrogenized vaginal smears until their seventh decade.

The relative significance of peripheral and central hormonal effects on sexual desire in aging women remains largely uncertain. Decreased lubrication and vaginal atrophy due to low circulating estrogens may lead to dyspareunia and a secondary decrease in sexual desire. Masters and Johnson (22) have indicated that these peripheral changes are less likely to occur in women who engage regularly in sexual activity. It has been suggested, however, that sexual desire may decrease independently from trophic genital changes, but the central effect of hormonal factors in this decline remains to be studied (8). Presently, there is no evidence of a direct relation between estrogen or androgen levels and changes in sexual desire in aging women.

It would seem important to conduct prospective studies to evaluate concurrently sexual activity and biological parameters, including sexual desire as an independent dimension. In view of the variety of factors other than desire that determine sexual frequency, one should exercise caution before attributing to aging the decrease in sexual interest reported by some patients. These factors include availability of partner, cultural expectations, medical illnesses, and emotional stress.

Pregnancy and Lactation.   Although there are wide individual differences, most investigators have found a decline in sexual interest and activity during the third trimester of pregnancy. A variety of psychological and physical factors are likely to be involved and no convincing evidence of hormonal mediation in sexual desire changes during pregnancy have yet been provided. Reduced sexual interest and activity may continue for several months during the postpartum period. The role of lactation on sexual function has only recently been considered. Masters and Johnson (22) found that 47 of 101 women studied postpartum reported low sexual desire. However, the women who breast fed, although showing estrogen-deficient vaginas, reported more sexual interest and an earlier resumption of sexual activity than the women who bottle fed. This intriguing difference may be explained by a recent observation (10) that women who reported a loss of sexual desire and responsiveness during lactation had significantly lower circulating testosterone and androstendione than those who did not breast feed. Further studies are necessary to clarify the role of psychological and hormonal factors in sexual desire during pregnancy and lactation.

Medical Illnesses

Any medical condition associated with pain, distress, and generalized weakness is likely to exert a nonspecific effect on sexual desire and activity. These nonspecific actions are at times difficult to separate from the specific effects of diseases that impair the neurologic, hormonal, and metabolic substrates of sexual desire. The most frequently observed medical disorders that affect sexual desire are summarized in Table 1 and will be briefly discussed below. It deserves note that most of the available information is limited to men, a bias that has permeated sexological investigation until recently.

Neurological Disorders. Disorders of sexual desire occur more frequently in association with temporal lobe epilepsy than in respose to epileptogenic foci in other brain structures. The most frequent effect on sexual function is a decrease in sexual drive and activity (23, 24), although there have been reports of hypersexuality (25) and deviant sexuality (26). Depressed sexual desire may be accompanied by lack of erotic fantasies and sexual dreams and by an inability to reach orgasmic release. Based on animal studies, it has been postulated that excessive limbic neuronal activity suppresses sexual drive and behavior. There are inconsistent reports

Table 1   Medical Determinants of Low Sexual Desire

Neurologic Disorders
Temporal lobe epilepsy
Brain tumors
Parkinsonism
Hormonal Disorders
Primary hypogonadism
Hypogonadotropic hypogonadism
Hyperprolactinemia
Thyroid disorders
Addison's disease
Cushing's disease
Metabolic Disorders
Chronic hepatitis
Hepatic failure (cirrhosis)
Chronic renal failure
Diabetes

that unilateral temporal lobectomy tends to improve sexual behavior primarily through an increase in drive (25, 27). It is unlikely that the effect of epilepsy on sexual function reflects solely abnormalities in neuronal activity; exploration of mediating mechanisms should also consider developmental and psychological determinants as well as the effect of anticonvulsive medication.

Brain tumors and strokes may impair both sexual desire and coital frequency, and it has been reported that their suppressive effects are greater in patients with left hemispheric lesions (28, 29). The confounding effects of emotional depression, motor impairment, and cognitive factors have not been clearly delineated.

Patients with Parkinson's disease tend to have depressed sexual functioning, but the precise prevalence and pathogenesis remains unclear. Several potential factors could be responsible, particularly mental depression and impaired movements. Whether there is a more specific effect possibly related to a decrease in brain dopamine remains unknown. Despite reported increase in sexual desire following L-dopa administration to patients with Parkinsonism, there are, as yet, no well-documented studies demonstrating that dopamine facilitates sexual behavior in humans.

Hormonal Disorders. Diminished sexual desire is frequently noted in men suffering from various hypogonadal disorders. Male hypogonadism may be primary as a direct result of gonadal impairment or secondary to abnormalities in hypothalamic-pituitary function. In instances of primary hypogonadism, such as Klinefelter's syndrome, orchitis, and testicular atrophy secondary to vascular insufficiency, damage to the Leydig cells leads to low testosterone production and a compensatory increase in luteinizing hormone (hypergonadotropic hypogonadism). When the impairment occurs at the hypothalamic pituitary lavel, such as in cases of pituitary adenomas, parasellar tumors, and autoimmune pituitary disease, subnormal secretion of luteinizing hormone and testosterone are usually observed (hypogonadotropic hypogonadism). The behavioral consequences of hypogonadism are quite varied; in some men, sexual desire and a capacity for sexual performance may remain unchanged for years. Clinical experience suggests that factors such as age of onset of hypogonadism, level of premorbid sexual competency, the medical and psychologic state of the subject and the attitude of the sexual partner are of considerable importance in determining the extent of sexual impairment. At present, few studies have systematically assessed clinical, hormonal, and psychological factors in relation to various sexual behavioral dimensions in hypogonadal men.

Recent reports (30, 31) show an association between pituitary tumors, high serum prolactin concentrations, diminished testosterone secretion, erectile impotence, and depressed sexual desire. It is believed that the hypogonadism observed in men with hyperprolactinemia is secondary to decreased gonadotropic secretion. Administration of bromocriptine, a dopamine agonist, frequently lowers prolactin concentration, elevates luteinizing hormone and testosterone, and restores sexual desire and potency.

The relation of hyperprolactinemia to lack of sexual desire is illustrated by a patient recently evaluated. Mr. S. is a 57-year-old lawyer, newly married for the second time, who complained of a progressive decline in sexual desire beginning about two years ago. Lack of sexual desire was global and persistent, although occasionally interrupted by fleeting increases in sexual interest, during which he had satisfactory intercourse and ejaculation. Most frequently, however, when he attempted intercourse in the absence of desire, he experienced erectile difficulties. Initially, the problem had been thought as psychological because of a history of intermittent erectile impotence at times of marital upheavals and the development of desire loss in association with a traumatic marital separation. At the time of our evaluation, Mr. S. described his present wife as attractive and quite supportive but experiencing perplexity by his lack of "sexual charge" in response to her advances. He had previously consulted an internist who had found "borderline" levels of plasma testosterone, but administration of depo-testosterone had not increased his sexual drive.

A full medical evaluation revealed an empty sella syndrome on pituitary scan, a moderately elevated circulating prolactin (34 ng/ml), and azoospermia. Administration of bromocriptin normalized prolactin levels and resulted in a significant increase in sexual desire and normal erectile function. All these changes reversed to the pretreatment state when the patient discontinued bromocriptin because of its unpleasant side effects.

The mechanism of action of bromocriptine in the treatment of erectile disorders associated with hyperprolactinemia is not fully understood. It may have a central effect on dopaminergic mechanisms that mediate sexual drive or it may improve erectile capacity due to the increased testosterone secretion that occurs as prolactin levels decrease. It has been observed, however, that restoration of erectile potency may occur before normalization of circulating testosterone.

Thyroid disorders, both hyperthyroidism and hypothyroidism, are found associated with depressed sexual drive. In both instances, gonadal function and circulating luteinizing hormone, follicle-stimulating hormone, and gonadal steroids may be impaired. Although not commonly observed in clinical experience, Addison's and Cushing's diseases have also been reported as causative determinants of hypoactive sexual desire.

Little is known about the specific effect of endocrinopathies on female sexual functioning. It has been assumed, but not yet adequately evaluated, that endocrine disorders that result in depressed sexual drive in men may affect women in a similar manner.

Metabolic Disorders. Depressed sexual desire is frequently noted in patients with chronic hepatitis and cirrhosis. Testicular atrophy is a common occurrence; in these conditions the diminished testosterone secretion is aggravated by increases in circulating estradiol and sex hormone-binding globulin, which lead to a proportionately greater decrease in free testosterone.

Over 80 percent of patients in chronic renal failure and uremia show lack of sexual interest, erectile problems, and arousal and orgastic difficulties in women (32). Although hemodialysis and renal transplantation improve the metabolic state, they frequently do not ameliorate sexual function. In some patients, however, sexual interest may improve following hemodialysis while erectile capacity shows further impairment. The results of endocrine studies of patients under hemodialysis have been variable; pituitary gonadotropins and prolactin are frequently elevated and circulating testosterone remains often below normal limits (33, 34).

The mechanisms mediating the effect of hepatic and renal failure on sexual function are likely to be complex. In addition to hormonal factors, they include neurologic disturbances, the influence of medications, and the effects of psychosocial stress and emotional depression.

Diabetes deserves mention as the most frequently encountered metabolic disorder. The lowering in sexual desire occasionally noted in diabetic patients is usually explained as being reactive to the erectile impairment frequently observed with these patients. Recent evidence (35) suggests that impairment of sexual desire may be, to some extent, independent from problems in sexual performance. This intriguing observation requires further study.

Pharmacologic Agents

The most frequent pharmacologic agents that impair sexual desire are listed in Table 2. As was the case with medical disorders, most of the reports on the effects of drugs on sexual functioning have been limited to men.

The drugs that most specifically influence sexual desire are

Table 2   Pharmacological Determinants of Low Sexual Desire

PRESCRIPTION DRUGS	DRUGS OF ABUSE
Endocrine Drugs	Alcohol
Cyproterone Acetate	Barbiturates
Medroxyprogesterone	Marijuana
Estrogen[a]	Narcotics
Antihypertensives	
Reserpine	
Alpha-methyldopa	
Clonidine	
Spironolactone	
Beta adrenergic blockers	
Psychoactive Drugs	
Phenothiazines	
MAO Inhibitors	
Haloperidine	
Benzodiazepines	
Antihistamines	

[a] In men.

antiandrogens and estrogen in men. Antiandrogens are substances that oppose the pharmacological effects of androgen through diverse mechanisms. Cyproterone acetate, for instance, a progestagenic substance that is used in the treatment of deviant sexuality, has antigonadotropic effects in addition to a competitive binding action at brain androgen receptor sites. Other synthetic progestagens such as medroxyprogesterone have also been used as antiandrogenic drugs based on their antigonadotropic effects. This results in a state of functional castration associated with a decrease in sexual desire and erectile impairment. Estrogen also induces a decrease in sexual desire in men, probably through a depression in testosterone production.

Antihypertensive drugs such as reserpine, alpha-methyldopa, clonidine, spironolactone, and beta-adrenergic blockers may depress sexual desire independently from their effects on erectile capacity. The pathophysiology involved is not clear because of their multiple mechanisms of action. It may include induction of central catecholamine depletion, sedative effects, and the development of a depressive mood.

Among psychoactive medications, phenothiazines, MAO inhibitors, haloperidine, and high doses of benzodiazepines may induce decreased sexual desire in both sexes. Again, it is difficult to speculate on the mechanisms that mediate their effects because of their multiple pharmacological actions. Phenothiazines, for example, are dopamine antagonists and alpha-adrenergic blockers, have antihistaminic and anticholinergic effects, and increase prolactin release. As previously discussed, impaired dopaminergic function and elevated prolactin secretion may have direct inhibitory effects on sexual desire.

Finally, among prescription drugs, antihistamines may also decrease sexual drive. It should be noted that there is a dearth of controlled prospective studies that have evaluated the effect of prescription medications on sexual desire independent from their action on sexual performance.

Drugs of Abuse

The deleterious effect of chronic alcohol intake on male sexual function is well known, but there is no clear evidence that alcohol has a specific inhibitory effect on sexual desire. In a series of long-term experiments reviewed by Wilson (36), it was documented that alcohol induced a dose-related decline of genital responses in both sexes. Learned expectations about alcohol effects, however, play a significant role in sexual interest and arousal, overriding the perception of physiological changes at times. The chronic effects of alcohol are complex and include inhibition of gonadotropic release and testosterone secretion, elevated estrogen levels, and neuropathic changes resulting in impaired tactile erotic sensations and erections (37).

Barbiturates and marijuana can also reduce sexual desire, depending on chronicity of use, dosage, and the subject's characteristics. As with alcohol, subject expectations play a significant role in individual responsiveness.

Among all drugs of abuse, narcotics such as heroin and morphine have the most consistent inhibitory effect on sexual drive in both sexes. The depressive effects on sexual desire are frequently reversible following drug withdrawal or a shift to methadone intake. The pathogenic mechanisms remain speculative, but possibly include depressed central nervous system function, physical debilitation, malnutrition, and diminished pituitary gonadal activity.

Depression

Loss of sexual desire is a well-recognized symptom of depression. The sexual impact of depression varies considerably, however, from person to person and is not always a reflection of the severity of the disorder as measured by independent criteria. Sexual desire may be impaired in the absence of erectile difficulties. It has been reported that whereas over 60 percent of depressed patients have impaired sexual interest, erectile dysfunction occurs in less than 33 percent of depressed patients (38, 39). In psychobiological investigations currently in progress, I have observed that subclinical depression is a frequent determinant of global and pervasive inhibitions of sexual desire. The effect of emotional depression on sexuality may be nonspecific, reflecting a lowering in well-being and energy, or it may be indicative of biochemical changes in brain amine processes that underly both mood and sexuality.

ASSESSMENT PROCEDURES

Psychosexual History

A detailed psychosexual history optimally involving both partners remains the cornerstone of an adequate evaluation of patients with disorders of sexual desire. From the standpoint of assessing possible biological determinants, several questions may provide valuable information.

1. Is the primary complaint loss of sexual desire? Is the complaint based on a change from the subject's previous level of sexual functioning, partner's expectation, or information about statistical norms?

2. Is the loss of desire global (occurs in relation to all potential partners) or selective?
3. Does the loss of desire encompass all forms of sexual expression (including masturbation and sex play as well as intercourse)?
4. Is the low sexual desire lifelong or does it represent a decline from a previous period of greater drive?
5. Is this loss temporarily associated with the development of medical illnesses, drug intake, or mood disorder?

Characteristically, when the loss of sexual desire is due to organic reasons, the problem develops progressively (with the possible exception of drug intake) from a previous level of satisfactory sexual functioning and manifests itself in a general and pervasive way. It is important to inquire whether the problem is primary or secondary to another sexual disorder such as impotence or premature ejaculation. This information is of critical importance for an adequate management of the patient. Finally, it is important to rule out during the psychosexual interview the existence of an underlying mood disorder that may be causally related to the lowering of sexual drive.

Medical and Laboratory Evaluation

A detailed medical examination including a history of drug intake, multichanneled blood chemistries, blood-sugar determinations (possibly including a glucose tolerance test), and hormonal assessments should complement the initial evaluation. The hormonal assessments should include testosterone (in men) and T_3 and T_4 analysis. Because of the well-known moment-to-moment variations in circulating testosterone, testosterone determination should be repeated if values are below normal (less than 3 ng/ml), along with determinations of blood luteinizing hormone and prolactin. Assessments of free testosterone and sex steroid-binding globulin are increasingly available and should also be considered. These procedures may determine the existence of a hypogonadal condition, whether the low testosterone is associated with a hyperprolactinemic state, and whether the hypogonadism is of central or peripheral origin. When appropriate, specialized tests such as a coronal CT scan and visual field studies should be obtained to rule out intracranial disease. Other specialized examinations should be requested as required to identify possible underlying medical conditions.

It should be emphasized before concluding that disorders of sexual desire reflect complex states that can best be understood by avoiding a dichotomous notion of biological versus psychological causation and by considering instead an interactive model that includes biological, psychological, and dyadic frames of reference.

References

1. Davidson JM, Camargo CA, Smith ER: Effects of androgen on sexual behavior in hypogonadal men. J Clin Endocrinol Metab 48:955, 1979

2. Skakkebaek NE, Bancroft J, Davidson DW, Warner P: Androgen replacement with oral testosterone undecanoate in hypogonadal men: a double-blind controlled study. Clin Endocrinol (Oxf) 14:49, 1980

3. Kwan M, Greenleaf WJ, Mann J, Crapo L, Davidson, JM: The nature of androgen action on male sexuality: a combined laboratory-self-report study on hypogonadal men. J Clin Endocrinol Metab 57:557, 1983

4. Bancroft J, Wu FCW: Changes in erectile responsiveness during androgen therapy. Arch Sex Behav 12:59, 1983

5. Schreiner-Engel P, Schiavi RC, Smith H, White D: Sexual arousability and the menstrual cycle. Psychosom Med 43:199, 1980

6. Schreiner-Engel P, Schiavi RC, Smith H, White D: Plasma testosterone and female sexual behavior, in Proceedings of the 5th World Congress on Sexology. Edited by Hoch Z, Lief HI. Amsterdam, Excerpta Medica, 1981

7. Bancroft J, Sanders D, Davidson D, Warner P: Mood, sexuality, hormones and the menstrual cycle III. Sexuality and the role of androgens. Psychosom Med 45:509, 1983

8. Bancroft J: Endocrinology of sexual function. Clin Obstet Gynaecol 7:253, 1980

9. Davidson JM, Kwan M, Greenleaf WJ: Hormonal replacement and sexuality in men. Clin Endocrinol Metab 11:599, 1982

10. Bancroft J: Hormones and human sexual behavior. J Sex Marital Ther (in press)

11. Everitt BJ: Cerebral monoamines and sexual behavior, in Handbook of Sexology. Edited by Money J, Musaph H. Amsterdam, Excerpta Medica, 1977

12. Benkert O: Pharmacological experiments to stimulate human sexual behavior, in Psychopharmacology, Sexual Disorders and Drug Abuse. Edited by Ban et al. Amsterdam, North-Holland, 1973

13. Pfeiffer E, Verwoerdt A, Wang, HS: Sexual behavior in aged men and women. Arch Gen Psychiatry 19:753, 1968

14. Verwoerdt A, Pfeiffer E, Wang HS: Sexual behavior in senescence. Geriatrics 24:137, 1969

15. Martin CE: Factors affecting sexual functioning in 60–79-year-old-married males. Arch Sex Behav 10:399, 1981

16. Stearns EL, MacDonnell JA, Kaufman BJ, Padua R, Lucman TS, Winter JSD, Faiman, E: Declining testicular function with age, hormonal and clinical correlates. Am J Med 57:761, 1974

17. Baker AWG, Burger HG, deKretser DM, et al: Changes in the pituitary-testicular system with age. Clin Endocrinol (Oxf) 5:349, 1976

18. Harman SM, Tsitouras PD: Measurement of sex steroids, basal luteinizing hormone and Leydig cell response to human chorionic gonadotropin. J Clin Endocrinol Metab 51:35, 1980

19. Davidson JM, Chen JJ, Crapo L, et al: Hormonal changes and sexual function in aging men. J Clin Endocrinol Metab 57:71, 1983

20. Weizman A, Weizman R, Hart J, et al: The correlations of increased serum prolactin levels with decreased sexual desire and activity in elderly men. J Am Geriatr Soc 31:485, 1983

21. McLennan MT, McLennan CE: Estrogenic status of menstruating and menopausal women assessed by cervico-vaginal smears. Obstet Gynecol 37:325, 1971

22. Masters WH, Johnson VE: Human Sexual Response. Boston, Little, Brown and Co., 1966

23. Gastaut H, Collob H: Etude du compartement sexuel chez les epileptiques psychomoteurs. Ann Med Psychol (Paris) 112:657, 1954

24. Blumer D, Walker AE: The neural basis of sexual behavior, in Psychiatric Aspects of Neurological Disease. Edited by Benson DF, Blumer D. New York, Grune & Stratton, 1975

25. Blumer D: Hypersexual episodes in temporal lobe epilepsy. Am J Psychiatry 126:83, 1970

26. Kolarsky A, Freund K, Machek J: Male sexual deviation: association with early temporal lobe damage. Arch Gen Psychiatry 17:735, 1967

27. Taylor DC, Falconer MA: Clinical, socioeconomic and psychological changes after temporal lobectomy for epilepsy. Br J Psychiatry 114:1247, 1968

28. Kalleomaki J, Markanen TK, Mustonen VA: Sexual behavior after cerebrovascular accident. Fertil Steril 12:156, 1961

29. Ford AB, Orfirer AP: Sexual behavior and the chronically ill patient. Medical Aspects of Human Sexuality 1:51, 1967

30. Franks S, Jacobs HS, Martin N, Nabarro JDN: Hyperprolactinaemia and impotence. Clin Endocrinol (Oxf) 8:277, 1978

31. Lundberg PO, Wide L: Sexual function in males with pituitary tumors. Fertil Steril 29:175, 1978

32. Kolodny RC, Masters WH, Johnson VE: Textbook of Sexual Medicine. Boston, Little, Brown and Co., 1979

33. Lim VS, Fang VS: Retardation of plasma testosterone levels in uremic men with clomiphene citrate. J Clin Endrocrinol Metab 43:1370, 1976

34. Hagan C, Olgaard K, McNeilly AS, Fisher R: Prolactin and the pituitary-gonadal axis in male uraemic patients on regular dialysis. Acta Endocrinol (Copenh) 82:29, 1976

35. Jensen SB: Diabetic sexual dysfunction: a comparative study of 160 insulin treated diabetic men and women and an age-matched control group. Arch Sex Behav 10:493, 1981

36. Wilson GT: Alcohol and human sexual behavior. Behav Res Ther 15:239, 1977

37. VanThiel D, Lester R: The effect of chronic alcohol abuse on sexual function. Clin Endocrinol Metab 8:499, 1979

38. Beck AT: Depression: Clinical, Experimental and Theoretical Aspects. London, Staples Press, 1967

39. Woodruff RA, Murphy GE, Herjanic M: The natural history of affective disorders, I: symptoms of 72 patients at the time of index hospital admission. J Psychiatr Res 5:255, 1967

3

Evaluation of Inhibited Sexual Desire: Behavioral Aspects

Joshua S. Golden, M.D.

3

Evaluation of Inhibited Sexual Desire: Behavioral Aspects

The outstanding sexual behavior common to all impaired sexual desire is sexual abstinence or avoidance. Whether that comes at the beginning of a sexual problem or follows later on in the course of the development of the symptoms is, of course, highly relevant. There is no such thing as a pure "organic" condition that leads to impairment of sexual desire or any other sexual dysfunction. One may have pure psychological problems, that is, sexual dysfunction caused purely by psychological factors. But any patient experiencing an organic problem is going to have a predictable series of psychological concomitants that complicate the behavioral manifestations of the problem.

The loss of sexual interest can result from a wide variety of psychological causes ranging from profound neurotic processes and serious relationship difficulties to simple performance anxiety and sexual ignorance in basically healthy persons who are in sound relationships. A detailed assessment of the patient's or couple's current sexual experiences and interactions yields such important information regarding the causes of the complaint that no evaluation in this area is complete without such a behavioral analysis.

There are six major categories of behavioral manifestations that help to evaluate and discriminate among the various psychogenic causes of impaired sexual desire: (a) performance anxiety, (b) relationship conflicts, (c) culturally induced sexual inhibition, (d) variation in sexual object choice or practice, (e) fears of pregnancy or sexually transmitted diseases, and (f) sexual phobias. The first two categories are the most common; the others are infrequent, although still significant.

Performance anxiety is a familiar phenomenon to most of us by now. The central nervous system balances inhibitory and facilitory systems, which explains how sexual desire can be facilitated through psychological phenomena. Unfortunately, most of us are familiar with how distraction of anxiety can inhibit sexual functioning.

A clinical example of the role of performance anxiety in impaired desire was a couple who presented with the complaint of low sexual frequency and loss of desire on the part of the man. The man was a very successful, driven advertising executive in his early 40s. For some months he had been unable to get an erection consistently. His wife, misinterpreting that symptom as perhaps an indication of his not liking her or not finding her attractive, began to put more and more demands on him to function sexually. The more he tried to function under this pressure, the more he began to experience impaired erection. A typical pattern developed. The man, because of his concern about getting an erection, would rush into sexual intercourse as soon as there was any appearance of an erection. His partner was not ready for penetration, and their sexual interactions became more and more unsatisfactory. A typical cycle of failure ensued. His anxiety about his performance interfered with his performance, which created more anxiety. As almost inevitably occurs when there are sexual difficulties, this couple's communications about sexuality were inadequate, and the problem became more and more painful. Human beings have the understandable tendency to avoid pain. The man began to turn off his desire to protect himself from the pain of humiliation and failure. The defensive inhibition of sexual desire does not occur on a conscious level, nor is it a voluntary act. The diminished sexual desire made psychodynamic sense, however, because it was preferable not to try at all than to try and fail, and risk humiliation and his partner's rage.

Nonsexual relationship conflicts are interesting in their own right and may exert a deleterious effect on a couple's sexual desire. The behavioral manifestations of relationship conflicts are particularly striking in that the block is selective. The impaired sexual desire is specific to a given individual, usually the spouse, and the person with the complaint of impaired sexual desire may experience normal sexual desires and function well when masturbating, or with a partner other than the one about whom there is ambivalence.

Among the less common problems is culturally induced sexual inhibition. There are people who have been taught that sex is bad and sexual pleasure is bad. That can be a very powerful, enduring message that exerts its pathologic effects notwithstanding all of the other messages, currently prevalent, that support a more permissive attitude.

An example was a couple where the husband complained that his wife, a woman in her mid-30s, would rarely, if ever, have sexual relations with him. Her sexual rejection of him had been a significant problem in the 10 years of their marriage. She had been raised in a fundamentalistic religious background that very strongly proscribed any kind of sexual activity and sexual pleasure. She had avoided sex whenever possible in the context of an otherwise loving and compatible relationship with her husband. Every few weeks, when her guilt over his discomfort would mount to the point that she would allow him to have sex, she would be, interestingly enough, easily, rapidly, and predictably orgasmic on clitoral stimulation as well as on intercourse. Unhappily, she would hate herself and would hate her body for experiencing that pleasure. Such cultural factors as this are becoming less prevalent, but they exist. Fortunately, there is a relatively good prognosis. These patients may benefit significantly from an encouraging attitude on the part of the therapist, who is more permissive than the authoritarian, inhibiting parental figures that they have known.

Variations in sexual object choice, preference, or practice are an important cause of low sexual desire when the patient attempts to have sex with a partner or in such a manner that is incompatible with sexual interests. This dynamic may explain impaired sexual desire toward an ostensibly appropriate partner. Recently, a successful attorney in his early 40s, who had been married for a number of years and who had one small child, came with his wife seeking sex therapy for his impaired sexual desire. He confided, when interviewed separately from his wife, that he had been troubled all his life by homosexual fantasies and inclinations on which he had never acted. Following a prolonged psychoanalysis in his mid-20s, he began to date women, had sexual relationships with a woman who was a very compliant, agreeable, and nondemanding person, and married her. They had one child. They had sexual relations very infrequently, usually on vacations and her birthday. The sex, not uncommonly, went without any problems in terms of physical functioning. There were no specific dysfunctions but the experience was not pleasurable for him. Characteristically, the couple communicated beautifully about everything but avoided the obviously important issue in evaluating their situation; namely, whether the husband might have a sexual preference other than for a heterosexual partner.

The fifth category, fear of pregnancy or of sexually transmitted diseases is mentioned because it is still a problem occasionally. Although it now seems that knowledge of contraceptive methods is readily available, fear of pregnancy is a possible cause of wishes to avoid coitus. Although the bacterially caused sexually transmitted diseases are easily avoided, or easily treated if contracted, herpes and acquired immune deficiency syndrome (AIDS) are neither, and fear of them is a frequent cause of impaired desire for sexual activity. An analysis of the sexual behavior of this type of patient reveals that sexual activities are enjoyable in all areas except those that would expose the person to what is feared. Thus desire is blocked in any situation potentially leading to pregnancy, AIDS, anticipated dyspareunia, and so on. When the encounter approaches the feared activity (e.g., coitus) or the mixing of sexual excretions, as in the case of AIDS, one finds a selective sexual inhibition and avoidance.

The sixth category is sexual phobia. There is a type of phobia that seems to have a physiologic element. It is manifest early in life, and may be associated with spontaneous panic attacks (1). It is particularly important to diagnose panic syndromes because such phobic patients are specifically treatable with a variety of antipanic drugs. The tricyclic antidepressants, alprazolam, and the monoamine oxidase inhibitors have been reported to be effective in blocking anxiety and panic attacks. The therapist may then deal with the secondarily developed avoidance responses that protect the person against the panic. Among patients who manifest sexual phobias and avoidance, it is necessary to differentiate between simple sexual phobias, which are amenable to treatment and psychotherapy alone, and phobias with an underlying panic disorder, which may require medication to block sexual panics in combination with psychosexual therapy (2, 3).

TYPICAL PATTERNS OF SEXUAL BEHAVIOR

Some patients with inhibited sexual desire exhibit some of the behavioral patterns clearly. There are also some typical patterns that are characteristic for the six different categories. The recognition of these patterns of sexual behavior during the evaluation provides important clues to the dynamics of the clinical problem, and also points to specific therapeutic interventions in assessing the patient or couple with inhibited sexual desire. Patterns of sexual functioning, noncoital affectionate behavior, anticipatory sexual anxiety, disinhibition by drugs, fantasy, and extrarelationship sexual activity are relevant areas of inquiry.

Sexual Functioning

When performance anxiety plays a significant role, there is characteristically a history of dysfunction during sexual activity. For this reason, it is appropriate to ask the patients in detail whether they are having problems with attaining or maintaining erection, achieving lubrication, experiencing orgasm, or any of the other criteria of adequate sexual function. With nonsexual conflicts in the relationship, there may not be a particular dysfunction during sexual activity. What is interesting about this pattern is that although patients may have no desire to be sexually involved with their partner, once they do become sexually involved, they frequently function without difficulty. Similarly, in the case of culturally induced sexual inhibitions, there may or may not be any impairment in terms of sexual response, depending largely on the extent to which the patient's sexual physiology is more healthy than the psychological effects that inhibit response.

Impaired desire due to variations in sexual object choice or practice ordinarily does not cause patients to experience dysfunctions. They primarily avoid sexual activity, although none of these patterns is absolute. With a fear of pregnancy or sexually transmitted disease, the pattern of avoidance is the clue. If the patients are engaging primarily in sexual intercourse, coitus, or some other sexual activity that is feared, their sexual functioning will depend on whether their fear is large enough to interfere with their ability to respond. With sexual phobia, the panic is so severe that there is really little likelihood that the patient is going to be able to function sexually, and the patient typically avoids physical sexual opportunities and may become depressed and obsessed about sexual avoidance.

NONCOITAL AFFECTIONATE BEHAVIOR

The absence, presence, and quality of a couple's noncoital affectionate behavior is of interest. Specifically, is the couple affectionate with one another and do they engage in physical and emotional behaviors short of sexual activity or coitus, or do they avoid all physical contact. Frequently, where performance anxiety is a major problem, there is a good deal of noncoital affectionate behavior. The couple likes one another; they are frequently involved in touching, kissing, and hugging, but avoid specifically that circumstance that may lead to sexual failure and performance pressure. When there are conflicts in the relationship, and the partners are hostile or ambivalent toward each other, there is less noncoital affectionate behavior. Noncoital affectionate behavior is not usually found in culturally induced sexual inhibition because such people tend to think that any affectionate behavior may turn into a sexual interaction. In such cases, the sexual avoidance occurs much earlier in the course of the contact.

Where there is a variation in sexual object choice or practice, there is frequently an absence of much affectionate behavior; the relationship may be very amiable albeit asexual. When the cause of impaired desire is fear of pregnancy or sexually transmitted diseases, one frequently finds a good deal of affectionate behavior. The couple may like one another and be strongly attracted. Avoidance is specific to activities that lead to the possibility of the "danger." The pattern varies with sexual phobia. Often one sees a relative absence of noncoital sexual affection because this may lead to the phobic situation.

ANTICIPATORY SEXUAL ANXIETY

Another relevant behavioral manifestation is that of anticipatory anxiety. Patients might be asked, "When you begin to think about the possibility of a sexual encounter, do you experience any anxiety? Are you apprehensive? Are you thinking about all of the possibilities that can go wrong—whether you won't get an erection, whether you won't lubricate, whether your partner is going to get angry, whether your partner is going to misunderstand?" Commonly, a therapist may observe that as patients hear this litany of thoughts, which often go through the minds of those with performance anxiety, they begin to nod their heads in assent and recognition because these mental processes are highly predictable. There is a great deal of anticipatory anxiety when performance anxiety is causing the impaired sexual desire. Where there are nonsexual relationship conflicts, the patients ordinarily have no intention of being sexually involved with their partner, even though they might be able to do so if they wanted to. As a result, anxiety is the exception in this patient population. Anticipatory anxiety is present when there is culturally induced sexual inhibition. With variation in choice of sexual object, anxiety tends to be absent because, like couples in conflict, the partners are not planning to be sexually involved. There is a good deal of anticipatory anxiety when the problem is the fear of pregnancy or sexually transmitted diseases. Of course, a great deal of anticipatory anxiety marks cases of sexual phobia.

EXTRARELATIONSHIP SEXUAL CONTACTS

If the patient is having sex with someone other than the partner, it is important to compare the patient's sexual response to the identified partner with sexual behavior outside that relationship. Frequently, in the case of performance anxiety, an individual will attempt sexual contacts with others to see whether he or she can be more successful than with the partner with whom there is difficulty. Not uncommonly, a person will attempt sex with another person in the hope that the dysfunction can be overcome. It is important to ask about extramarital sex, although it is necessary to do so discreetly, preferably in a separate individual session.

In the case of nonsexual relationship conflicts, sexual relationships with others may be quite satisfactory. This is also true when the relationship is harmonious but the patient has an intimacy conflict that prevents experiencing erotic desire within the context of a committed relationship. Typically, in the case of culturally induced sexual inhibitions, there are no sexual relationships with anyone. Should the patient attempt this, he or she will not be able to function. When there is a variation in sexual object choice or practice, there may be a history of sexual behavior with a person who represents the desired sexual object (e.g., a homosexual partner) or a history of engaging in the sexual practice that is desired (e.g., pedophilia). In the cases of sexual phobia and of fears of pregnancy or sexually transmitted diseases, there are no extrarelationship sexual contacts.

SEXUAL FANTASY

Sexual fantasy is frequently used by people with performance anxiety as an attempt to get them over their inability to function sexually. Those patients who have nonsexual relationship conflicts frequently fantasize about somebody else with whom sexual relationships would be more enjoyable or less threatening. Where there are culturally induced sexual inhibitions, sexual fantasy is rarely used. Paradoxically, inhibited patients frequently have a very rich sexual fantasy life, which tends to be reciprocal and in some way related to the extent of their inhibition. The more inhibition, the richer the fantasy life. However, fantasies are rarely used in the context of a relationship with a partner. In fact, conscious withholding of fantasy is a readily modified cause of inhibited sexual desire. Where there is a variation in sexual object choice and practice, sexual fantasy is very frequently employed. Generally, the fantasies involve the uncommon, forbidden, or unacknowledged sexual object or preference. When the problem is fear of pregnancy or sexually transmitted diseases, there is no particular relationship to the use of sexual fantasy. Sexually phobic patients are generally too distressed to use imagery or sexual fantasy.

RESPONSE TO DRUGS: DISINHIBITION

An interesting aspect of behavior is whether there is disinhibition, that is, some greater amount of sexual appetite, when the person has been influenced by drugs or alcohol. With performance anxiety, one occasionally observes greater sexual desire and activity when mildly intoxicated, although it is not a consistent finding. A person who gets drunk or uses marijuana or other chemical releases may be able to perform much more successfully, although the drug-induced improvement is rarely consistent.

In nonsexual relationship conflicts, one does not tend to see release of sexual behavior. People with a culturally induced sexual inhibition, like those with performance anxiety, are frequently able to function sexually and quite well only when they are intoxicated or when their inhibitions are suppressed. That same behavior in response to drugs may also be seen, albeit somewhat more inconsistently, when there is a variation in sexual object choice or practice. Fear of pregnancy or sexually transmitted diseases are rarely going to be influenced by drugs or alcohol. In the case of sexual phobia, where there may be some mitigating effect from antianxiety drugs or alcohol, long-range beneficial effects of antipanic drugs are likely only if the antidepressants, the monoamine oxidase inhibitors, and alprazolam are used therapeutically.

RESPONSE TO SEX THERAPY EXERCISES

The patient's response to the prescription of sex therapy exercises may sometimes help to discriminate among the causes of impaired desire. When inhibited sexual desire is secondary to performance anxiety, patients are initially hesitant to engage in sexual prescriptions. If they continue in therapy, however, they generally become more active and enthusiastic and respond in a positive manner. In cases where there are nonsexual relationship conflicts, patients do not usually respond well to the therapy exercise. In fact, such patients may be expected to react negatively to any experience that promotes closeness. They are very highly resistant and find innumerable reasons not to engage in the program. When there is culturally induced sexual inhibition, they may frequently be initially resistant, although with some degree of motivation. If the patients are responsive to a permissive authority figure, who encourages them to be sexual and can somehow convince them with their partner that sexual activity is an appropriate "good" thing for them to do, then there may be a cooperative response to the behavioral prescriptions. Where there is a variation in sexual object choice or practice, it is ordinarily not the case that patients are going to be very responsive to behavioral prescriptions, except to those that encourage the use of the variant fantasy. Some people may be more amenable to change of their sexual object preference. There have been some reports, albeit few, that these patients may do well with sex therapy exercises. Where the fear is one of pregnancy or sexually transmitted diseases, if that fear can be realistically dealt with by proper contraception or prophylaxis against sexually transmitted diseases, then the patients are going to be quite cooperative. Where there is a sexual phobia, there is likely to be an aversive reaction to the prescription of sexual behavior unless antipanic medication is used to block the panic reaction.

References

1. Klein DF: Anxiety reconceptualized, in Anxiety: New Research and Changing Concepts. Edited by Klein DF, Rabkin JG. New York, Raven Press, 1980, pp 235–241

2. Kaplan HS, Fyer AJ, Novick A: The treatment of sexual phobias: the combined use of anti-panic medication and sex therapy. J Sex Marital Ther 8:3–28, 1982

Suggested Reading

Kaplan HS: The Evaluation of Sexual Disorders: Psychological and Medical Aspects. New York, Brunner/Mazel, 1983

4

Evaluation of Inhibited Sexual Desire: Psychodynamic Aspects

Otto F. Kernberg, M.D.

4

Evaluation of Inhibited Sexual Desire: Psychodynamic Aspects

To discuss the inhibition of sexual desire in terms of severe character pathology or personality disorders, it is necessary first to offer a summary of the development of normal sexual behavior.

PSYCHOSEXUAL DEVELOPMENT

Psychoanalytic investigation has highlighted three broad levels of psychosexual development as the source of fantasies, conflicts, and behaviors. In the first stage, the preoedipal stage, the capacity for sensual excitement linked to erotogenic zones and to skin eroticism appears. There is also a development of polymorphous perverse infantile sexual tendencies that we reencounter in the "paraphilias" or sexual deviations or perversions in adults. There is a difference, however, between infantile polymorphous perverse strivings and subsequent perversion. Normal polymorphous infantile sexuality is multiple in its interests—shifting and flexible —in contrast to the restricted, obligatory, rigidly repetitive nature of sexual fantasies and activities in sexual deviations.

The sexual impulses linked with the oral, anal, and genital zones and with skin eroticism find expression in the child's fantasies involving relations with the preoedipal and oedipal objects. But the sexual, erotic quality of these infantile fantasies is also mixed with aggressive fantasies—the derivatives of aggressive impulses. Sadistic and masochistic, in addition to voyeuristic and exhibitionistic, homosexual and heterosexual strivings and fantasies are all combined in various forms. The sexual object itself, in this preoedipal stage of development, is less important in its intrinsic qualities than as a way of gratifying sexual desire.

The polymorphous quality of these sexual fantasies shifts significantly during the second stage of development, the oedipal stage. In this stage, genital impulses, particularly toward the parental objects, become predominant. There is the characteristic triangularization of the oedipal situation, both positive and negative. With the establishment of object constancy, the culmination of the stage of separation-individuation that predates the oedipal stage of development, the child enters the oedipal stage. What is of importance here is the predominance of genital interests and the extent to which the preoedipal polymorphous sexuality becomes integrated into it. The childhood objects, the parental figures, are perceived as differentiated not only from each other, but especially in their sexual features. Parents, siblings, and others are perceived in an integrated fashion, with their positive and negative aspects combined. Children now have so-called total or global object representations of these people, in contrast to only partial images of them as "all good" or "all bad" that characterize the sexual fantasies of the earlier psychosexual stage of development.

The typical sexual fantasies derived from the oedipal phase maintain their triangular quality throughout life. We find this, for example, in the normal sexual fantasy life, in the fears of being displaced by a sexual rival, or in the particular interest of a woman for a man who is involved with another woman. The wishes to be involved with or pursued by two persons from the other sex is another frequent fantasy, a reversal of the infantile situation in which the child was competing in fantasy with the parent of the same sex for the sexual interest of the parent of the opposite sex. These triangularizations are maintained with varying degrees of disguise both in sexual behavior and fantasy throughout life.

The achievement of object constancy signals the capacity for experiencing love and hatred toward the same person. This integration, carried into the oedipal stage of development, permits the experience of ambivalence—of both loving and hateful feelings toward the oedipal object—and the predominance of love in the relationship. Aggression is not dangerous because it is contained by a loving relationship.

A third developmental stage is the postoedipal phase. Its successful completion signals the achievement of the preconditions for normal adult sexual functioning from a psychodynamic viewpoint. This phase represents the integration of three categories of intrapsychic functioning. The first precondition is the preservation of polymorphous perverse infantile strivings that are maintained as sexual foreplay and as polymorphous perverse sexual fantasy, which is a crucial aspect of erotic art, pornography, and the sexually exciting aspects of sexual fantasies that enrich—expressed in actual behavior—genital intercourse per se. Polymorphous perverse sexual fantasy is a crucial contributor to the intensity of sexual excitement. This sexual excitement should facilitate the experience of orgasm. The experience of orgasm also requires a tolerance for a temporary merging with another, a tolerance that derives from the earliest experiences of self-object merging of infancy.

This temporal sense of merging with the other person is very difficult, if not impossible, to tolerate for some borderline patients with relatively frail ego boundaries, in whom a sense of merger represents a danger of loss of ego boundaries. This sense of merger in the experience of orgasm is normally enriched by the intense sexual excitement with the orgasm of the sexual partner, which reflects the unconscious activation of homosexual strivings linked with the negative oedipus complex—the identification with the parent of the other sex. The normal intense sexual excitement with the excitement and orgasm of the sexual partner of the other sex, and the merger experience in fantasy that signifies a tolerance of temporary self-object refusion reminiscent of the infantile symbiotic phase of development are preconditions for a normally rich sexual excitement and orgasm.

Thus normal sexual fantasy includes not only genital but also polymorphous perverse sexual fantasy and the capacity for and tolerance of corresponding behaviors as well. Such fantasies and behavior should also tolerate certain derivatives of aggression so that the normal individual should be able to tolerate and integrate sadistic and masochistic fantasies and behaviors in sexual inter-course. A typical normal fantasy is that of using the other person as an "object," or of being "used" as an object—thus satisfying sadistic (in the first case) or masochistic (in the second) impulses while feeling secure because love in the relationship provides a frame that safeguards the total sexual relation.

In short, the ability to accept polymorphous perverse derivatives of infantile sexuality is the first precondition for normal sexual experience. In patients with relatively mild sexual difficulties deriving from disturbances in the oedipal stage of development, we often find a capacity for stable object relations and stable sexual relations, but an impoverishment of the intensity of sexual experience per se because unconscious prohibitions against pre-oedipal derivatives manage to eliminate through repression the derivatives of primitive polymorphous perverse fantasies and play.

A second precondition for normal sexual relations from a psychodynamic viewpoint is the capacity to achieve an object relation in depth. According to psychoanalytic theory, this means the tolerance of ambivalence (of both aggressive and sexual and loving feelings) toward the same person, the capacity to under-stand and empathize in depth with another person, and the availability of an integrated concept of the self. These characteris-tics of an object relation in depth (or a "total" object relation) go hand-in-hand with the capacity for tenderness and sharing. The capacity of an object relation in depth is typically lost in narcissis-tic personality disorders. In fact, we have been able to study the characteristics of normal love relations and sexual pleasure by exploring their absence in those patients.

Clinically, the lack of a capacity for object relation in depth means that the sexual relation with a partner cannot be integrated with an emotional investment in the partner. This impoverishes sexual experience. It brings about sexual boredom and frustration, and an endless search for new partners. Normally, a gratifying sexual relationship intensifies interest in the sexual partner. In narcissistic pathology, sexual gratification leads to an almost obligatory loss of that interest.

Normal object relations are characterized by ambivalence. The risk is that the intensity of the aggression toward the person, who is at the same time loved, may destroy the relationship. Sexual intimacy means the activation of normal, significant conflicts around ambivalence and the potential intense activation of early oedipal and preoedipal conflicts in sexual relations. Normality, then, does not mean absence of conflicts.

A third precondition for normal sexual relations is the integration of a normal superego. The unconscious, infantile, internalized sense of morality and values related to the consolidation of the superego replaces, on the positive side, the earlier self-esteem regulation by means of external admiration, praise, and punishment by a more stable internalized guidance system. On the negative side, however, the superego may cause severe sexual inhibitions by the pathological maintenance of infantile sexual prohibitions that eventually interfere with normal sexual experiences in adolescence and adulthood. The superego has both positive and negative effects on the sexual life of the individual. On the positive side, the superego leads to the idealization of the sexual partner, the capacity to fall in love, to remain in love, and to experience concern for the other person. It enriches and consolidates the stability of the couple that derives from their capacity for an object relation in depth.

Normally, important transformations take place within the superego in adolescence so that sexuality is reinstated while the oedipal prohibitions, in a narrow sense, are reconfirmed. This optimal development often does not occur, and an excessively strict and sadistic, infantile superego remains, determining that, while object relations can be maintained in depth and the capacity for falling in love and remaining in love is preserved, this occurs at the heavy cost of an unconscious inhibition or repression of sexual functioning. This is a major cause of inhibition of sexual desire.

SEXUAL PSYCHOPATHOLOGY

The corresponding pathology is linked to the stages of development outlined and can be roughly classified into three levels of severity.

Inhibition of sexual desire appears as a symptom in some severely narcissistic, paranoid, and schizoid personalities—personality disorders within the spectrum of "borderline personality organization." In these cases there is an inability to establish object relations in depth of such a severity that the individual remains practically isolated and has enormous difficulties in establishing any sexual involvement. The narcissistic personality cannot because of the deterioration and depreciation of object relations. The paranoid personality cannot because of intense fears of any member of the opposite sex. The schizoid personality cannot because of a general fragmentation of affects. It should be stressed that only the most severely narcissistic, paranoid, and schizoid personalities show this inhibition of sexual desire, yielding a poor prognosis.

A second, milder level of sexual pathology can be found in the ordinary personality disorders that function on a borderline level: (a) the infantile, hysteroid, or histrionic personality; (b) the narcissistic personality; (c) the schizoid personality; and (d) the paranoid personality. This level is characterized by sexual promiscuity and a capacity for normal genital functioning and enjoyment of sexual intercourse, but with a simultaneous incapacity to establish an object relation in depth. Therefore, the interpersonal relations of these patients seem dissociated from their sexual behavior. These patients may present promiscuous or polymorphous perverse sexual behavior, or particular sexual deviations. They do not present an inhibition of sexual desire. They usually have severe conflicts in intimate relations as a consequence, among other reasons, of the dissociation between sexual behavior and emotional investment. This dissociation is caused not only by the difficulty in investment in object relations in depth, but also by the lack of normal superego development they frequently present.

A third, milder level of sexual pathology includes patients who have achieved a normal integration of object relations with the corresponding capacity for the establishment of object relations in depth. These patients have integrated the early, polymorphous perverse infantile stage of psychosexual development. They have also achieved consolidation of ego identity and of superego integration. They have the capacity to fall in love, to remain in love, and to be invested in depth in others. This, however, is at the cost of sexual inhibitions of varying degrees of severity.

We find this particularly in two personality types: the hysterical personality (not to be confused with the infantile, hysteroid, or histrionic personality disorder in DSM-III, its regressive counterpart) and the depressive–masochistic personality. (Unfortunately, these two personality disorders have been left out of the corresponding section of DSM-III.) These two personality disorders represent, together with the obsessive–compulsive personality, the better functioning, "higher level" or "neurotic" personality disorders. It is in patients with hysterical personality and with depressive–masochistic personality that we very frequently find inhibition of sexual desire.

Clinically speaking, hysterical psychopathology is illustrated by the cases of men who have to dissociate their sexual behavior into a "madonna–prostitute" dichotomy, and who can be sexually active and potent only with women they depreciate. They are either not interested in or have an inhibition of sexual excitement or orgasm with women they idealize. Corresponding hysterical psychopathology in women is illustrated by patients who can be orgastic with men who mistreat them, but not with men who respond to their love. These women can be orgastic with a lover but not with a husband. These are women with selective inhibitions of sexual desire that follow typical triangular patterns reflecting underlying oedipal conflicts.

Another disorder of sexual desire, pseudohypersexuality, is usually a symptom of personality disorders. These are patients whose sexual activity is in excess of what is expected for their age and culture. They show an incapacity to maintain interest in a sexual partner over an extended period of time and, simultaneously, are excessively active sexually. Psychological exploration reveals that these patients are lacking in sexual satisfaction. Although their sexual functioning itself is normal enough, the pervading satisfaction from sexual intercourse is absent. These are usually patients with narcissistic personality disorders.

EVALUATION

In diagnostic evaluation we first have to investigate sexual fantasy, activity, and dreams to evaluate total sexual activity. The patient's sexual orientation, wishes, and conflicts may be expressed only in masturbation fantasies, in homosexual or heterosexual activity, or in daydreams and fantasies. Rarely, only dreams give us clues to dominant sexual interests and conflicts.

In any case, when the total range of polymorphous perverse fantasy or activity is rich and included in actual heterosexual intercourse, and when actual sexual activity is rich and creative, we are confronting normal sexual behavior. When infantile polymorphous perverse sexual elements are inhibited so that sexual intercourse is confined to its genital aspects, we are probably in the presence of an oedipal type of pathology. We have to evaluate the internal freedom of fantasy and behavior present in sexual intercourse, the integration of aggression into it, and any discrepancy between unconscious and conscious sexual orientation (this is important in patients with inhibition of sexual desire). For example, a man may wish to have intercourse with women but he is not actually interested in intercourse with women (an inhibition of sexual desire); his dreams may have exclusively homosexual contents. He may be terribly threatened by conscious homosexual fantasies or feelings, but his dream life may indicate a contradiction between conscious wishes to become sexually excited with women and his unconscious fantasy life. In addition, sexual fantasy, particularly masturbation fantasies, very often give us crucial clues to the dominant sexual conflicts and inhibitions, including inhibited desires.

Second, we have to evaluate the quality of object relations. This can be achieved by studying whether the patients are able to describe themselves in depth, and whether they can describe the most important people in their life in depth, particularly the person with whom they are involved sexually. This capacity, to have a concept of oneself and of the other person in depth, indicates that there is no identity diffusion (or that there exists normal identity integration). By the same token, it helps to diagnose the severity of the pathology responsible for the inhibition of sexual desire. If the patient presents a capacity for maintaining object relations in depth, this reinforces the probability that we are dealing with an oedipal level of sexual pathology, which means the patient has a better prognosis than a patient whose inhibition has preoedipal roots.

Third, we have to evaluate the quality of superego functioning. Is there a capacity for normal idealization processes, for falling in love? Narcissistic patients typically have difficulties falling in love or remaining in love. Is there a capacity for concern and commitment to another person? Is there any evidence of excessive unconscious prohibitions against sexuality, such as shown in sexual naiveté and sexual ignorance? Cultural and religious prohibitions very often interface with unconscious infantile superego-determined prohibitions. Generally speaking, a harsh but well-integrated superego is a prognostically favorable feature for treatment of inhibitions of sexual desire, indicating pathology stemming from the oedipal level.

Fourth, we have to evaluate the total relationship with the sexual partner, including the stability and depth of the actual object relation of the couple; the harmony of their cultural commitments, ideals, and aspirations; and unconscious mutual identifications. A man and a woman may come from different cultures and have severe cultural conflicts. They may have different aspirations and goals regarding their marriage. They may unconsciously project parental images onto the other and reenact conflicts unresolved from early developmental phases. Obviously, if they have severe conflicts at all three levels of their cultural background, their personal aspirations, and mutually enacted unconscious conflicts, the relationship will probably not last. But conflicts at one or two of these levels may be tolerated and expressed in a chronically conflictual yet stable relationship, and may result in inhibition of sexual desire.

For example, although a couple may be "very much together" culturally and in terms of their personal aspirations, there may exist an unconscious activation of repressed past internalized object relations projected onto the partner that unconsciously makes the partner and the relationship very dangerous and frightening. The mechanism of projective identification may unconsciously activate in the partner frightening conflictual relations from the past that inhibit sexual behavior—a factor related more to the psychopathology of the couple than to intrapsychic factors in the strict sense mentioned before.

Fifth, we have to evaluate the actual sexual behavior of the couple, including their freedom in sexual play and their interests in mutual sexual involvement. This involves evaluating the presence of excessive superego features—which very frequently show in mutually induced inhibitions—so that both partners would consciously like to be sexually freer, but project their own superego onto the partner, who then acts as the reenactment of their own infantile prohibitive superego. Marital conflicts and misunderstandings may reinforce psychodynamically caused inhibition of sexual desire by three mechanisms: (a) by superego collusion, the mutual reinforcement of unconscious prohibitions; (b) by a masochistic submission to aversive sexual behavior of the partner, reflecting, for example, a masochistic–depressive or hysterical personality; and (c) by using sex as a general battleground for displaced conflicts from other origins.

Concerning the indications and contraindications for treatment, from a psychodynamic and general psychotherapeutic viewpoint, we have to evaluate the motivation for change of both partners and the secondary gain derived from an inhibition of sexual desire (e.g., unconscious acting out of aggression toward the sexual partner). We also need to study the indications and contraindications for the three dominant modalities of treatment for psychodynamically determined inhibition of sexual desire: individual psychotherapy or psychoanalysis, sex therapy, and marital therapy. For practical purposes, individual psychotherapy or psychoanalysis, sometimes combined with marital therapy, is probably the predominant modality of treatment for psychodynamically determined inhibition of sexual desire.

In sum, first, we must consider the level of personality organization. The prognosis is very good for neurotic patients (neurotic in terms of neurotic personality organization) with good identity integration. Prognosis is poor for those narcissistic patients who have inhibition of sexual desire. Prognosis is intermediary for schizoid and paranoid personalities with inhibition of sexual desire. Second, we have to explore the secondary gain provided by the symptom; for example, the predominance of intense revengeful wishes against the sexual partner or a sense of superiority over the partner gained by sexual rejection. The greater the secondary gain, the poorer the prognosis. Third, we should evaluate the unconscious sexual needs defended against. If they are of a nature that would be extremely threatening to the patient's conscious experience and self-concept, or very difficult to bring up in the treatment without seriously threatening the present equilibrium in the patient's life, the prognosis is less favorable.

As a psychoanalyst, a psychotherapist, and a psychiatrist, I have found it extremely helpful to work jointly with sex therapists and family therapists or marital therapists in evaluating difficult cases and difficult couples. Frequently the problem is not so much the diagnosis but the treatment. A team approach involving a psychodynamic or psychoanalytically oriented psychotherapist, a marital therapist, and a sex therapist can enormously improve our total scope, depth, and intensity of treatment.

Suggested Readings

Kernberg OF: Barriers to falling and remaining in love. J Am Psychoanal Assoc 22:486–511, 1974

Kernberg OF: Mature love: Prerequisites and Characteristics. J Am Psychoanal Assoc 22:743–768, 1974

Kernberg OF: Boundaries and Structure in Love Relations. J Am Psychoanal Assoc 25:81–114, 1977

5

Evaluation of Inhibited Sexual Desire: Relationship Aspects

Harold I. Lief, M.D.

5

Evaluation of Inhibited Sexual Desire: Relationship Aspects

To evaluate or treat a sexual dysfunction, especially inhibited sexual desire (ISD), the clinician must pay particular attention to the quality and dynamics of the patient's relationship with spouse or other partner. The interpersonal dimensions of a dysfunction often prove to be the dominant factor in its etiology and maintenance. Perhaps a brief anecdote will illustrate this:

Husband: Why don't you ever tell me when you have an orgasm?
Wife: You're never around.

Let's face it: to put it bluntly, a penis does not make love to a vagina. Love requires two interacting people. Therefore, in addition to the biological, behavioral, and intrapsychic dimensions, the therapist has to consider carefully the interpersonal aspects.

BRIEF HISTORICAL OVERVIEW

The field of sex therapy is an amalgam of individual, couple, and behavioral therapy. Up to about 1950, individual therapy was about the only approach to the treatment of sexual dysfunction. The following decade witnessed the development of family therapy under the leadership of Nathan Ackerman, Don Jackson, and others. Marital or couple therapy developed a body of concepts and skills, especially in the 1960s and 1970s. The two fields are growing closer in both theory and practice, and the merger between them is now almost complete. During the past two decades, behavioral therapy has made similar strides. Increasing numbers of clinicians claim behavioral therapy as their primary orientation.

Probably more than all the psychotherapies available today, sex therapy integrates marital and individual therapy, and synthesizes psychodynamic and behavioral concepts and practices. Moreover, it also integrates medical and psychiatric (or psychological) methods of evaluation and treatment.

FIVE COMPONENTS OF HUMAN SEXUAL RESPONSE

Kaplan (1) was correct when she criticized and amplified Masters and Johnson's (2) early two-phasic approach to the diagnosis and nosology of sexual dysfunctions. This early simple formulation divided the dysfunctions into disorders of excitement or of orgasm. Kaplan added the desire phase, which is under consideration in this monograph. The triphasic approach has been an enormous improvement leading to more accurate diagnosis and treatment procedures. Additional clinical and research experience requires modification once again. To aid the understanding of the five components of the human sexual response, I have coined the acronym DAVOS: desire, arousal, vasocongestion, orgasm, and satisfaction. Desire must be distinguished from arousal. The excitement stage is separated into two components, one psychologic (arousal) and the other physiologic (vasocongestion). The psychologic component of excitement is not always accompanied by its physiologic component. A classic example is impotence, in which there may be intense arousal and a diminished physiologic response. Conversely, it is possible to have a physiologic response without the full range of arousal. A case in point is that of a woman who is being physiologically monitored for perivaginal, uterine, and anal contractions during excitement and orgasm who shows the full range of sexual response, clearly indicating orgasm, but fails to label the experience as such. Heimann (3) has reported that as many as 15 percent of women may fall into this category.

Just as arousal and vasocongestion are not always synchronized, and therefore have to be regarded as separate components of excitement, so too orgasm and satisfaction may be desynchronized —hence the need to have a separate component evaluating the quality of satisfaction. A person may go through the full range of human sexual response and derive little satisfaction from it, usually because of negative feelings toward the partner or the situation in which sex occurs. On the other hand, it is possible to have a limited sexual response without orgasm and be well satisfied. This is often true of women who find their greatest satisfaction in the closeness and intimacy of the encounter. Much more emotional weight may be attached to the feeling of sharing and connectedness than to the erotic experience itself. Men, being more genitally oriented, are somewhat less likely to separate the total psychological experience from the quality of the erotic one.

THE SIGNIFICANCE OF THE DESIRE PHASE

Although desire phase disorders have been described and discussed much more thoroughly in the last few years than ever before, and have assumed greater prominence in the minds of professionals treating sexual dysfunctions, it is erroneous to think that this discovery is entirely of recent origin. In 1949, Rado (4) spoke of the "internal stimulation" that establishes a receptivity to sexual cues or signals. He may have been alluding to nonreporting neural activity that underlies the sexual drive, as well as the awareness of being excited. In the absence of internal scripting for sexual activity, the cognitive aspect of the internal stimulation, a "sexual motive state" fails to be established. In Rado's view, it is this sexual motive state "which mobilizes and organizes the organism's emotional and other resources for orgastic pleasure." It is the combination of this internal stimulation (including neurophysiological brain activity and scripting) and the sexual motive state that comprises the desire phase of the human sexual response.

It is not altogether clear from Freud's writings that he included a desire phase in the sequence of events. He speaks of a "turning away of the libido" (5) at the initiation of the act, but by this he probably meant an inhibition of arousal rather than of desire.

EVALUATION OF INTERPERSONAL CAUSATION OF INHIBITED SEXUAL DESIRE

If a person has ISD from any cause, biologic or intrapsychic, it is certain to have an effect on a marriage, unless the partner shares the same lack of interest in sex. The resulting marital conflict often enhances ISD and the situation tends to worsen. However, this common situation is not our main concern. The focus is not on marital conflict as a cause of maintaining ISD; rather it is on those dyadic interactions that cause ISD in the first place.

The key point in the case history that should lead the clinician to think of interpersonal factors as the primary determinant of this dysfunction is if the ISD is situational or, to be more specific, partner-related. If the person did not have ISD with other partners, then it is very likely to be connected to problems in the relationship. There are exceptions. These exceptions occur in people with intrapsychic conflicts that are expressed in a close intimate relationship, most typically marriage. For example, a man with a "madonna–prostitute" complex makes an unconscious association between his mother and his wife, and the incest taboo will inhibit his lust for the incestuous object, now his wife rather than his mother. So strong is the taboo that he divides women into two classes, one pure and virtuous, hence nonsexual, and the other degraded, sexually interested, and interesting. Lust is for the latter category of woman, whereas love is reserved for the virtuous and asexual woman. This man develops the same inhibition in succeeding marriages, so it is not the unique relationship per se that causes hypoactive desire. This state of affairs is common, so common that Freud termed this "the most prevalent form of degradation of the erotic life"(6).

A parallel situation is found in women, although less frequently. I can recall a young woman, much attached to her father, who was very passionate with her fiancé premaritally, but whose

Table 1 Male Psychosexual Disorders: Comparison of First and Second Field Trials, in Percent

	First (N = 61)	Second (N = 72)
Inhibited Sexual Excitement (Impotence)	39%	42%
Premature Ejaculation	26	14
Inhibited Sexual Desire	20	14
Other Diagnosis: Not Classified Elsewhere	15	8
Inhibited Male Orgasm (Retarded Ejaculation)	. . .	6
Marital Problem	. . .	15

passion disappeared entirely on their wedding night. She continued to have a passionless existence until, in exasperation, her husband insisted on separation. Since in every other way he loved his wife, he agreed to sleep with her on the night they had announced their separation to their family and close friends. To her great surprise, and to him as well, she was as passionate as she had been prior to marriage.

There are other intrapsychic causes of situational ISD. Men and women who are afraid of intimacy may similarly be unable to develop desire for someone with whom they have a committed relationship. Fear of intimacy may have different causes and may take many forms. Examples include the inhibition of aggressive sexual impulses toward the love-object, and fear of dependency on or loss of the partner. One of its consequences can be a decrease in sexual desire, although it often takes the form of an inhibition of excitement or of orgasm. In that case, ISD is often a secondary and eventual consequence of the other dysfunction.

Although "situational" partner-related hypoactive desire usually points to the dyadic factors as a cause, the clinician should not overlook the possibility that significant intrapsychic conflict is being expressed in the marriage. To add to the complexity of the subject, dyadic interactions may represent not only "real" conflict in the relationship, but the projection of intrapsychic forces onto the partner and the distorted perceptions that result. One example, described by Dr. Kernberg in Chapter 4, is the projection of a person's superego onto the partner, creating the erroneous impres-

Table 2   Female Psychosexual Disorders: Comparison of First and Second Field Trials, in Percent

	First (N = 54)	Second (N = 35)
Inhibited Sexual Desire	37%	31%
Inhibited Female Orgasm	28	20
Inhibited Sexual Excitement	13	3
Marital Problem	· · ·	17
Major Affective Disorder (Depression)	· · ·	11
Dyspareunia	6	· · ·
Vaginismus	2	· · ·
Not Classified Elsewhere	15	11
Other Diagnosis	· · ·	7

sion that the partner is uninterested in sex or objects to certain sexual practices. How much weight to attach to transferences within the marriage, and how much to the dyadic "misfit," is a therapeutic task that is an important factor in reaching a decision about whether to recommend individual or couple therapy.

FREQUENCY OF INHIBITED SEXUAL DESIRE

In testing the diagnostic categories of DSM-III, two field trials were run at the Marriage Council of Philadelphia several years apart. In these field trials, we took successive patients with a sexual diagnosis and determined which dysfunction was the primary or original problem. This was modified in the second field trial by adding marital problems as a primary diagnosis. Table 1 shows the frequency of psychosexual disorders in men. In the first field trial, ISD occurred in 20 percent; in the second field trial, ISD occurred in 14 percent. The drop in the percentages of both premature ejaculation and ISD in the second field trial took place presumably because some of those cases were now labeled as marital problems (as the primary diagnosis). Many of these patients had ISD as a secondary diagnosis.

The frequency of psychosexual disorders in women in the first and second field trials is shown in Table 2. ISD was the most frequent diagnosis in both field trials, although there was some-

Table 3 Frequency Distribution of Psychosexual Disorders Among 107 Men and Women in a Second Field Trial

Diagnoses	Number of Diagnoses (%)			
	Men (N = 75)		Women (N = 35)	
Inhibited Sexual Desire	20	(16)	18	(24)
Inhibited Sexual Excitement	42	(33)	8	(11)
Inhibited Female Orgasm	...		15	(20)
Inhibited Male Orgasm	7	(5)	...	
Premature Ejaculation	15	(12)	...	
Atypical Psychosexual Dysfunction	2	(2)	7	(9)
Not Classified Elsewhere	4	(3)	1	(1)
Marital Problems	26	(20)	16	(21)
Paraphilias	3	(2)	0	
Anxiety Disorders	1	(1)	2	(3)
Affective Disorders (Depression)	8	(6)	7	(9)
Paranoia	0		1	(1)
Totals	128	(100)	75	(100)
Average per Patient	1.78		2.14	

Note. No cases of dyspareunia, vaginismus, or ego-dystonic homosexuality were diagnosed.

what of a drop in the second field trial when marital problems was added as a primary diagnostic category. The occurrence of depression in 11 percent in the second field trial undoubtedly decreased the diagnosis of ISD as well.

Multiple diagnoses are shown in Table 3. The men had 1.78 diagnoses per patient; the women had 2.14 diagnoses per patient. Restricting the diagnoses to the psychosexual dysfunctions, one can see that ISD was the most common of diagnoses in women. Although ISD represented only 24 percent of all the diagnoses in women, it actually affected more than half the patients (18 of 35). Although ISD represented only 16 percent of all the diagnoses in men, it still was present in almost 28 percent of the patients. In men, ISD was primary in 14 percent and secondary in 14 percent. In women, ISD was primary in 24 percent and secondary in 27 percent. From these figures, one could predict that ISD would be evenly divided between primary and secondary diagnoses in a sex therapy clinic.

My recent patient data discloses that in 1982, I saw 155 "patient-units" (couples or individuals) with whom I had had at least one consultation. Of these, 120 presented with a sexual problem and 30 (25 percent) with ISD. Of the 30 units, 6 patients came alone and 24 came as couples. This meant that I saw 54 people whose lives were complicated by ISD, either in themselves or in their partners. Of the 24 couples, there were 6 in which both partners had ISD, and 18 couples in which only one partner had ISD. This meant that I was dealing with 36 patients with ISD, 20 men and 16 women.

COUPLE ETIOLOGY OF INHIBITED SEXUAL DESIRE

Just as we lack a biogenic marker for ISD, we also lack a psychogenic one. There is no one thing that we can point to in order to differentiate an intrapsychic case from an interpersonal case. Of the 30 units with ISD, clinical judgment (and that is the only thing one can rely on) led to the appraisal that half the units were mostly intrapsychic. This means that the primary reason the couple was having trouble around hypoactive sexual desire was an intrapsychic problem. The 6 cases that presented alone were primarily intrapsychic. In the 24 couples, the intrapsychic and interpersonal factors were approximately equal. There was an intrapsychic problem in one or both partners in 9, it was mostly interpersonal in 9, and approximately equal in 6. This demonstrates the dovetailing of intrapsychic and interpersonal factors, and it highlights the frequent difficulty in separating the two major dimensions of psychogenicity.

Before turning to some cases illustrating some of the diagnostic problems, I would like to present a brief review of some of the major dimensions of marital dynamics. The major components of marital relationships are marital boundaries, power and control, and intimacy. Conflict over the intrusion of in-laws and other family members, work, children, recreational pursuits, community activities, religious activities, and lovers and friends causes anger on the part of the spouse who feels neglected, and guilt on the part of the spouse who is following extramarital interests and allowing them to intrude on the marital boundaries to the spouse's discomfort. Both anger and guilt can markedly decrease sexual desire. A case in point is that of a young woman who was very angry with her husband, who, overly influenced by his mother, called his mother every day and often discussed his wife and disclosed marital secrets. The wife had lost all interest in sex.

Similarly, if there is a competitive struggle and an attempt on the part of each partner to dominate the other, the struggle for power and control may be overt. Frequently, however, one finds the struggle for power and control to be covert, with one person using passive–aggressive techniques, managing to provoke enough guilt in the partner to be able to assume control through manipulation, or controlling the situation by inducing protection and nurturance. An example would be that of the chronic invalid who induces both protection and guilt, creating in the nurturant spouse a lot of counter-erotic hostility inhibiting sexual desire.

The other significant area of marriage is intimacy. *Intimacy* is too broad and nonspecific a term to be clinically useful. It can be operationalized and made useful therapeutically by breaking it down into its components: (a) affection, (b) autonomy, (c) commitment, (d) companionship, (e) conflict-resolution, (f) expressivity, (g) identity, (h) respect, (i) sexuality, and (j) trust. Of these, studies have demonstrated that the most important dimension is expressivity, or the capacity to share one's thoughts and feelings with the partner. The sharing has to be a two-way street, involving the capacity to listen to one's spouse as well as the ability and willingness to express oneself. Without intimacy, the spark goes out of the relationship, eventually seriously affecting sexual desire. Any feelings of disappointment over any of the aspects of intimacy can eventually produce hypoactive sexual desire. If a person is distrustful because of a real or fantasized extramarital relationship, desire for sex can wane. Similarly, if one person is treated with disrespect, the anger caused by this may adversely affect sexual desire.

Generally speaking, the intervening variable between marital conflict and ISD is any of the so-called emergency emotions—fear, anger, guilty fear, and guilty anger. On occasion, this can be pseudo-anger. For example, a woman who had professed great irritation with her husband and said he was the reason for her inhibited desire was really using this as an excuse. She was having a torrid extramarital affair and needed to have a reason to avoid sex with her husband. Although genuine guilty anger was present to some degree, she exaggerated her anger to ward off her husband's sexual advances. She also demeaned and derogated him to such an extent that he was usually impotent, which conformed to her secret wishes. Usually the anger is not feigned; it is real and is a consequence of conflict over marital boundaries, power, control, or some frustration of the wish for intimacy.

ILLUSTRATIVE CASE HISTORIES

Marital conflict over marital boundaries, power and control, or intimacy may produce hypoactive sexual desire in either partner. The most striking example of marital boundaries being threatened is that of an extramarital sexual relationship. Still, it is not always easy to predict which partner will have hypoactive sexual desire. It can be the person who is enamored of the third party, or it can be the aggrieved partner who is made so angry that sex becomes impossible. In many instances the marriage is terminated not because of the wishes of the partner who strays, who in many instances would prefer to keep the marriage intact, but because this partner finally gives up in exasperation when the injured spouse repeatedly turns a cold shoulder. After months, or even years, of this treatment, the marriage ends in divorce. In those situations, it is sometimes difficult to tell who is being victimized.

In one respect, at least, it does not matter if the hypoactive sexual desire is a consequence of marital conflict per se or if the difficulty between the partners is really generated by intrapsychic factors finding expression in transference reactions or projective identifications, or even a defense against sadomasochistic or other paraphiliac fantasies and impulses. The marital unit must be looked at as a system requiring the transactional approach found in systems analysis. The following cases in which one or both partners had ISD illustrate the systems approach.

A couple in their late 20s presented with bilateral ISD. The hypoactive sexual desire was more pronounced on the part of the husband, but the wife's interest in sex was largely limited, and based on her stated desire to have a child. Married for five years, they had had intercourse no more than a half dozen times in those five years. Six or seven months might go by without an attempt at intercourse. This was in striking contrast to their passionate relationship during their courtship. Their passion was cut short immediately after the formal announcement of their engagement. That night, the bridegroom suddenly lost all interest in sex, a reaction that was not resisted to any great extent. They were married six months later, and had had practically no sexual contact in that six-month period.

At first, their response to sensate focus was so gratifying that the therapist at first believed that this would be an easy case to cure. Resistance to sensate focus began a week after they had successfully completed stage one. At that point, the therapist began to dig more deeply into the backgrounds of both partners. Therapy was broken off as resistance increased, but several months later the couple returned for individual sessions, at which time additional data were obtained. It turned out that the husband was the last child of many siblings. When he was a young teenager, he was finally informed of a deep dark family secret: that a brother who was about 17 years older than the patient had impregnated a sister two years younger than the brother. All this had taken place when the patient was an infant. When he learned about this as a young teenager, it apparently left the unspoken idea in his head that "it's not safe or proper to have sex with a relative."

The wife, with considerable resistance, finally related her family secret. Her father had made six or eight abortive attempts to bed down his daughter. She recalls, for example, one evening when she returned to the house after a date, that her father had scolded her in front of her date, embarrassing her greatly. When the date left, he had embraced her, and she could feel his erection through his pajamas. Similar things happened a number of times. Once in a movie theater he had tried to fondle her thigh and touch her vagina. She had resisted all his efforts, but had felt excited by them. Apparently the bride and bridegroom learned the same message, but in somewhat different ways. "One musn't have sex with a relative" developed enormous power when the two of them became formally engaged.

It is always intriguing to think that people with interlocking neurotic patterns, patterns that reinforce and maintain the dysfunction, can find each other.

Another example of intrapsychic factors being expressed in a couple beset by interacting pathology was that of a 36-year-old professional woman in a two-career marriage. The couple presented because of the wife's marked inhibition of sexual desire that developed into a phobic avoidance of sex. She had grown up in a household dominated by a father who would scream and yell at the slightest provocation and would brook no disobedience from his children. The patient, the only daughter, grew up intimidated by her dominating and extraordinarily controlling father. She married a man who was very gentle and kind, and yet at the same time quite stubborn. He was a very shy and nonaggressive lover, which bothered the wife who wanted a more sexually assertive person. The sexual assertion must not go too far, however, because she had a marked fear of loss of ego boundaries during intercourse, a terrible fear of being controlled and dominated by her husband, and a greater fear of controlling and dominating him because the last thing she wanted to do (consciously) was to behave like her father. She could neither submit to an aggressive male, nor could she take over the aggressive role because she had a fear of devouring and absorbing him through her vagina. The husband, who would become very upset if he became angry, would resist most attempts to get him to be more sexually assertive. This left the wife uncertain about his love and desire for her. Still, her husband's passivity played into her fantasy, and she felt somewhat safe. In therapy, however, she made every effort to get her husband to be more assertive. Her sadistic conception of sex led to greater fears when she had control in her own hands than in allowing power to reside in her husband's.

The following case history illustrates the conjunction of intrapsychic conflict with interpersonal dynamics.

A businessman in his late 50s, married to a woman 10 years younger, had had ISD for approximately 15 years. This was so extensive that sexual relations occurred only three or four times a year. The wife put up with this state of affairs for many years because she secretly had had a very active, dynamic man as her lover. She managed to meet him about once a week and had managed to keep her affair a secret from her much more passive husband. Finally, her guilt increased and, at her suggestion, her husband came with her for treatment. He was very resistant to sensate focus exercises, indicating his conflict over resuming a sex life with his wife. He could come up with no idea why he had this severe inhibition. In one session following a sharp argument with his wife, he brought up a dream in which he was lying on a beach when a very aggressive blond woman (his wife was blond) came by and seized him by the hair and dragged him along the beach. His association to the dream was that he had fleeting impulses to be tied down hand and foot to the bed while his wife would do what she wished with him. These fantasies were so disturbing that he would put them out of mind as quickly as they would occur to him. Indeed, he hadn't thought of this fantasy for months until it had been stimulated by the dream. This illustrates a case of repression and suppression of an impulse that had to be warded off by completely turning off the desire for sex. There was complicity in this by his wife, who used this as an excuse for her extramarital affair.

The clinician will see cases in which life cycle changes alter the dynamics of the marital system.

A 29-year-old physician married to a woman several years older had lost sexual desire for the last year and a half. He had married his wife while a medical student, very much attracted to an extremely competent and effective woman who rapidly rose to an executive position in her firm. The security engendered by the wife's competence began to be less important to the physician as he became successful in his own right, and he began to resent the higher status of his wife and her extraordinary competence. In essence, he was moving from a child–parent relationship, present at the beginning of the marriage, to one in which he wanted to achieve equality. This was enhanced by his growing stature and position at the hospital. A female intern, very much attracted to this young physician, was successful in seducing him. He fell in love with her, but was wracked with guilt. In the meantime, his sexual desire for his wife declined enormously. His decreasing interest in sex with his wife was enhanced by the so-called age 30 crisis in which he was evaluating his life, what he had accomplished, and where he wanted to go. Therapy was successful in maintaining the marriage, which seemed to be about to dissolve. The real value of the relationship was recognized once more as the partners worked through the change in role relationships over time.

Marital transferences stemming from previous reactions to parents create perceptual distortions and maladaptive interactional behavior.

A couple in their late 30s presented with bilateral ISD. The wife would avoid sex entirely, except when her husband initiated it, which was rare. She did it as a form of obligatory sex with the desire to please him without deriving much pleasure in the encounter. His desire was at a low ebb, and had been for some years. He believed that his wife was incapable of sexual response and was put off by her apparent use of sex as a means of pleasing him rather than a form of mutual enjoyment.

The history of this couple is of interest. The husband was raised in a family where the father was very busy and neglected his family, especially his son. The son never felt that he could get his father's attention or interest. He was attracted to a fellow graduate student who had an unusual interest in her work, frequently spending Saturday nights in the library. She came from a family where her mother had been completely dependent on the father, who had been rather cruel and inconsiderate of the female members of the family. Her parents had had a master–slave relationship. The daughter vowed that she would never be dependent on a man, and so developed a career in which she became a highly paid consultant to industry.

When this couple married, despite her misgivings about depending on her husband, the wife reached out with affection and tenderness. These attachment interactions were rejected by her husband. She withdrew and devoted herself to work. As she became more and more of a workaholic, her husband became more resentful, and gradually lost whatever interest he had had in sex. Analysis of the situation revealed that he had married a woman who in some way would remind him of his father with the thought that he would be above and beyond hurt as the situation with his wife repeated the painful interaction with his father. Additionally, he had the unconscious thought that he could modify this script and force his wife to pay attention to him. In fact, his growing hostility toward her made her withdraw even more into her work, setting up a vicious circle of resentment, increased withdrawal, and increased resentment.

Good sexual functioning requires the fine tuning of verbal and nonverbal communications during sex and an effective feedback system permitting partners to sense and empathize with each other, modifying their behavior as needed. Attachment interactions can thus be fine tuned. Conflicts over sexual repertoire or dominance and submission in sex can be overcome by such fine tuning as not steering the partner into a certain activity when one senses resistance. The appreciation of this change can eventually modify the initial resistance. Sex can become very restricted and narrowly focused when the sexual value system is not only different, but leads to conflict, repetitive anxiety, and avoidance behavior. This restriction of sexual activity frequently leads to sexual boredom and hypoactive sexual desire. Partners must attend to the fine tuning of attachment and exploratory interactions to prevent or to overcome hypoactive sexual desire.

> A man in his early 30s married about six years after he had lost his fiancée in a plane crash. Fearful of commitment because of the fear of the loss of someone loved, he withdrew sexually. It was difficult for him to show affection as well as to engage in sex. His wife, instead of responding sensitively to her husband's fear of intimacy, became more and more angry. As her anger grew, he became more and more distant, and sex became less and less frequent. They did not achieve any capacity to fine tune their sexual and affectionate interactions until they came into treatment.

Verhulst and Heimann (7) also speak of territorial sexual interactions. Commonly, a man will believe his wife to be his "territory" and she may try to defend access to her own body as the man tries to take possession of it. This conflict can lead to mutual hostility and ISD. Sometimes, strangely, territorial interactions produce unusual combinations.

> A man in his late 50s came in with his wife for treatment of ISD. This was at her urging. At the time they came in for treatment, he had a mistress, which was causing the wife much pain and anger. It turned out there had been a repetitive pattern over the years in which the husband found it almost impossible to make love to his wife, but felt great passion in extramarital relations. Although there was a distinct madonna–prostitute component to the husband's ISD, a more significant feature was devaluation of anything he possessed, including his wife and children. His whole behavior was directed toward acquisition. He was a caricature of Fromm's "acquisitive personality" and in a sense resembled Don Juan, whose major interest was in conquest. The devaluation of his possessions was so marked that he would pay no attention to his business accounts unless there was some threat to them. He could go after new acquisitions and fight to maintain old ones, if threatened, but otherwise neglected anything that he had. This included the clothes on his back, even though he was an enormously wealthy man.

CONCLUSION

Sex therapy is a form of psychotherapy and requires that the therapist be a competent psychotherapist with an effective grasp of individual and marital dynamics. It is insufficient simply to know the behavioral aspects of sex therapy, although that is a sine qua non of sex therapy. It must be enhanced by the capacity to understand relations between families of origin and transferences within the marriage, the nature of communication and transactional patterns, and the ability to enhance individual and marital growth by modifications in the marital system. Sex therapy is not a simple task. It is a complex amalgam of individual and couple therapy, of behavioral and psychodynamic therapy, and of systems analysis. Hypoactive sexual desire is an important symptom, indicating that the system is malfunctioning.

References

1. Kaplan HS: Disorders of Sexual Desire. New York, Brunner/Mazel, 1979

2. Masters WH, Johnson VE: Human Sexual Inadequacy. Boston, Little, Brown and Co, 1970

3. Heimann J: Issues in the use of psychophysiology to assess female sexual dysfunction. J Sex Marital Ther 2:197–204, 1976

4. Rado S: An adaptational view of sexual behavior, in Psychosexual Development in Health and Disease. Edited by Hoch PH, Zubin J. New York, Grune & Stratton, 1949

5. Freud S (1926): The Problem of Anxiety. New York, WW Norton & Co, 1936

6. Freud S (1912): On the universal tendency to debasement in the sphere of love (Contributions to the psychology of love II), in The Standard Edition of the Complete Psychological Works of Sigmund Freud, vol

11. Translated and edited by Strachey J. London, Hogarth Press and the Institute of Psychoanalysis, 1957, pp. 178–190

7. Verhulst J, Heimann JR: An interactional approach to sexual dysfunctions. The American Journal of Family Therapy 7:19–36, 1979

Suggested Readings

Hoch Z, Lief HI (eds): Sexology: Sexual Biology, Behavior and Therapy. Amsterdam, Excerpta Medica, 1982

Lief HI (ed): Sexual Problems in Medical Practice. Chicago, American Medical Association, 1981

Lief HI, Hoch Z (eds): International Research in Sexology. New York, Praeger, 1984